ADVERTISING ACCOUNT PLANNING

ADVERTISING ACCOUNT PLANNING

PLANNING AND MANAGING AN IMC CAMPAIGN

SECOND EDITION

LARRY D. KELLEY

AND

DONALD W. JUGENHEIMER

M.E.Sharpe
Armonk, New York
London, England

Library of Congress Cataloging-in-Publication Data

Kelley, Larry D., 1955–
Advertising account planning : planning and managing an IMC campaign / by
Larry D. Kelley and Donald W. Jugenheimer.—2nd ed.
  p. cm.
Rev. ed. of: Advertising account planning : a practical guide. 2006.
Includes bibliographical references and index.
ISBN 978–0-7656–2563–2 (cloth: alk. paper); ISBN 978–0-7656–2564–9 (pbk.: alk. paper)

1. Advertising. 2. Advertising—Management. 3. Advertising campaigns.
I. Jugenheimer, Donald W. II. Title.

HF5823.K344 2011
659.1′11—dc22   2010022585

Printed in the United States of America

The paper used in this publication meets the minimum requirements of
American National Standard for Information Sciences
Permanence of Paper for Printed Library Materials,
ANSI Z 39.48-1984.

∞

IBT (c)   10   9   8   7   6   5   4   3   2   1
IBT (p)   10   9   8   7   6   5   4   3   2   1

Contents

Preface and Acknowledgments

Advertising Account Planning: Planning and Managing an IMC Campaign was designed for anyone charged with developing a comprehensive advertising campaign.

Account planning is a crucial aspect of the integrated marketing communications process yet little has been written on account planning in general and even less on how account planning affects each stage of the process. Our goal with the first edition of this book was to try to fill this void. We focused on the basics of account planning; what it is, where it came from, and the role it plays in advertising agencies. The second edition goes further.

Since the publication of the first edition, many changes have taken place in the world of advertising. The rise of digital marketing communications, the convergence of communications disciplines, and the rapid pace of change in the consumer environment are some of the major changes sweeping the industry. Account planning has changed as well. Account planning and/or account planners are now a part of public relations practices, digital agencies, and even client organizations in addition to the advertising agencies. Advertising account planning has a clear role in the full communications process. We also see this on the student side of the ledger by the changing aspects of the National Student Advertising Competition (NSAC), which hundreds of universities compete in annually through the American Advertising Federation (AAF).

This second edition is designed to be a guide for developing an integrated marketing communications campaign using account planning principles at each stage of the development process. Because of the importance of account planning within today's world of advertising and marketing, it makes sense to train future practitioners in its art and practice. This training may occur in formal advertising and marketing courses in colleges and universities, in training programs at advertising companies and agencies, or is learned on the job by those who need to use and apply account planning to their work situations. Thus we see this book as especially relevant for students who are taking an account planning course or participating in a campaigns course either through their college or university or through the NSAC competition. We also believe this book will serve the needs of new employees in the advertising business as well as more experienced advertising practitioners who want to use or understand account planning principles in their business and work.

Advertising Account Planning: Planning and Managing an IMC Campaign is not filled with theories, models, or equations. Instead, the book deals with the practical side of account planning and campaign planning. Specific examples are drawn from professional award-winning campaigns as well as student NSAC award-winning campaigns. The examples offer students and practitioners practical examples of how account planning is incorporated into integrated marketing campaign practice and development.

This second edition follows the logical development and execution of an integrated marketing campaign. After the initial chapters, which cover the history and role of account planning, we follow a campaign structure that begins with a discussion of the brand destination process that ties into a situation analysis. From there we discuss the role of research in determining what consumers think and feel about your brand. Within this aspect of the book, we also discuss what consumer insights are and how you can find them.

The following material is also new to this edition: A discussion of the role of advertising within the marketing challenge; current examples of target segmentation, brand positioning, brand personality, and an exploration of how to determine a brand's essence; an entire chapter dedicated to the concept of "the big idea" and how to tie it to a campaign; the briefing process throughout the campaign; and a chapter on the impact of account planning on various integrated marketing communication disciplines, such as media, public relations, and digital marketing. The book concludes with thorough discussions of the role of creative testing in advertising and measuring results of an integrated marketing campaign.

Review questions, discussion questions, and resources round out each chapter. These features help the reader review and understand the material.

The authors have published a number of widely used advertising materials. Larry D. Kelley has significant advertising agency experience in account planning and Dr. Donald W. Jugenheimer has many years of experience teaching college students a variety of courses, including advertising campaigns, advertising management, and advertising account planning. Both authors have been advisors to student NSAC competition teams and understand the role that account planning plays in this process. Together, their background and strengths have come together to provide a unified learning experience.

Use the book as it was intended: as a teaching and learning aid as well as a resource for those who actually practice the art and science of account planning.

Acknowledgments

The authors would like to thank the following persons and organizations for their help and support during the writing and editing of this book: Marjorie Sheriff, who worked diligently to coordinate research for the book and to get the manuscript into its final form; FKM agency, who provided insights into the content of the book; American Association of Advertising Agencies, Account Planning Group, International Practitioners of Advertising, and the AAF, who provided content and case studies for the book, and the individual agencies and universities that allowed us to use their case studies.

We owe a special thanks to Harry Briggs, our editor; Stacey Victor, our production editor; and Elizabeth Granda, who helped us negotiate the production cycle at M.E. Sharpe. We especially want to thank our spouses and families for all their support, without which this project would not have been feasible.

ADVERTISING ACCOUNT PLANNING

Chapter 1

Account Planning History and Practice

Every member of a company or organization can affect its success by enhancing its brand equity. Perhaps you are a brand manager responsible for a specific brand or portfolio of brands. Maybe you are the president of a company or the chief marketing director. Or maybe you are an account planner, account manager, or president of an advertising agency. Perhaps you are working on a campaign for your college or university to compete in the National Student Advertising Competition (NSAC). Regardless of your situation, how your brand or company is positioned and perceived in the marketplace is crucial to your success.

Positioning your brand and then determining how that positioning is to be executed in all forms of communication can be a daunting task even for the most seasoned professional. However, ensuring that the time you spend positioning the brand is properly accepted by all of the brand's stakeholders, whether within the company or among consumers, is vital to the ultimate success or failure of the brand. There is nothing more disturbing to a brand manager than for the advertising, the promotions, the public relations effort, and the digital effort to be misaligned. In today's complex world of communication, disconnects happen every day in hundreds of companies.

It can be a difficult task to pull together a brand's position and to get that position properly executed in all the appropriate marketing communications channels. The process can be confusing and sometimes elusive. The simple fact is, you cannot develop an integrated marketing communications campaign and hope to evaluate its impact on the brand without proper planning. The purpose of this book is to help bring clarity to the job of developing an integrated marketing communications campaign by linking the brand's positioning with communications. This task revolves around the art and science of account planning.

Account planning can be a job or a department, or it might be a process within an agency or within a marketing group. No matter how account planning is being handled on your brand, it is one of the most important aspects of placing the consumer at the heart of every decision you make for your brand and its communications.

Origins of Account Planning

Although the history of account planning has its origins in the United Kingdom, the reason for the rise and adoption of account planning is truly an international tale. Account planning came of age due to a variety of circumstances in the history of advertising.

In the 1950s, advertising agencies were the pioneers of advertising and marketing research. At that time, advertising agencies had large market research staffs or subsidiary companies that conducted marketing research. Agencies were the informational source for consumer behavior and attitudinal trends. For example, Leo Burnett in the United States had a marketing research staff that rivaled the top-20 research companies of that era. Investment in primary research allowed advertising agencies to act as consultants to their clients on all aspects of marketing and advertising. Large consumer marketing companies that promoted consumer packaged goods, automotive merchandise, and general goods and services relied on advertising agencies to tell them about their customers. The account manager of the advertising agency often filled the role that today's brand managers do in consumer products companies. Figure 1.1 shows a traditional advertising agency structure.

But this situation began to change in the 1960s when consumer products companies began moving from manufacturing or operations management systems to what we now know as the brand management system. Prior to this period, consumer brands or companies were headed by operations executives with limited marketing know-how. In the 1960s companies made a shift toward having marketing experts lead the charge. This period of transition began to change the relationship between the client and the advertising agency. The clients, now run by brand managers, brought market research into the company rather than relying on the advertising agency for the majority of consumer input. Brand managers wanted to devise their own research and saw the current agency/client system as cumbersome. This shift placed advertising agencies in more of a specialist role, working only on advertising instead of on all aspects of marketing. With consumer knowledge and understanding moving away from advertising agencies and to the client, marketing strategy also was the responsibility of the client rather than of the agency. Agencies struggled to cope with these changes.

In the late 1960s, two UK advertising agencies, Boase Massimi Pollitt (BMP) and J. Walter Thompson (now called JWT) started what we refer to

Figure 1.1   **Traditional Advertising Agency**

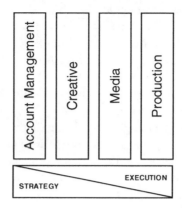

as *account planning*. However, while each of these agencies began the trend at a similar point in time, they came at it from very different directions.

BMP approached account planning through the research function. Research in their advertising agency, like most, was typically a backroom activity. The researcher would conduct research and pass it along to the account manager who would interpret the research for use on the client's business. BMP saw flaws in this system on a couple of fronts. First, the account manager was not a research expert and might not interpret the results accurately. Second, the account manager was sometimes too close to the account to be truly objective when dealing with consumer perceptions of the brand. Third, the account manager was torn between satisfying the client on one hand and providing creative direction on the other. So BMP developed an enhanced research role that placed the research department on equal footing with the account management and creative departments within the advertising agency. In essence, BMP brought research to the forefront within the process in an objective role between the account manager who served the client's needs and the creative group, which worked to develop messaging to influence the consumer. Stanley Pollitt envisioned the role as an "account man's conscience" and someone who would help direct creative strategy and determine how a campaign was measured.

At about the same time, JWT London merged its marketing department with its media and research departments and called it "account planning." Stephen King of JWT probably coined the term *account planning*. King saw a similar dilemma at JWT as did Pollitt did at BMP. However, King envisioned the account planner role more broadly than that of BMP. In the BMP model, the account planner would be more of a creative strategist working with the account manager and the creative department on creative strategy and ultimately campaign measurement. JWT London saw the account planner as having a much broader strategic planning role in advertising. At JWT, the account planner had a role in the complete advertising strategy, from defining the role that advertising plays in an account to target segmentation, media strategy, and brand positioning, as well as creative strategy and development.

Both agencies made changes in an effort to add consumer response to the client and creative viewpoints.

Advertising account planning began to take shape in the United Kingdom in the 1970s. Account planning groups were formed in the late 1970s to bring together a discipline that had various roots, practices, and criteria. It was highlighted in 1979 when England's Account Planning Association shifted its International Planning Awards for advertising from pretesting to the use of planning and strategy as a gauge for advertising effectiveness. This shift also set the stage for some account planners to break away and form their own advertising agencies. Clients quickly followed suit and supported this new type of agency oriented around planning.

Spread of Account Planning

Account planning didn't make its way to the United States until the late 1980s, almost twenty years after its introduction in the United Kingdom. Jay Chiat, the founder of the Chiat/Day agency, is credited with introducing account planning in the States. Chiat's reason for bringing an account planner to his agency was simple. He felt that more innovative and compelling advertising was being done in the United Kingdom than the United States at that time. He believed that account planning was the secret to this innovation. Chiat/Day was known prior to the introduction of account planning as a very creative advertising agency. After the addition of a UK account planner and the subsequent introduction of the famous 1984 Macintosh computer commercial and a string of impressive new business wins, other U.S. advertising agencies stood up and took note of this phenomenon.

Other U.S. advertising firms began to import UK account planners to their advertising agencies. One such account planner was Jon Steel, who migrated to Goodby, Silverstein & Partners, a fierce competitor of Chiat/ Day. Steel's success with Goodby, Silverstein & Partners and his 1998 book, *Truth, Lies and Advertising: The Art of Account Planning* put the world of account planning into the mainstream. Since the late 1990s, account planning has been largely adopted by advertising agencies within the United States and across the world.

Through the 1990s and into the 2000s, there have been other seismic changes in the advertising agency landscape. Media services that were once a part of a full service advertising agency were spun out as separate companies. The rapid rise of digital advertising has spawned a new set of advertising agencies that focus on this space. With the rise of social media and other new channels of communication, public relations is also being redefined. All of these changes have led to account planners adapting to new agency structures and environments. It is not unusual for media, digital, and even public relations agencies to have account planners on staff to add consumer insights or to serve as strategic leaders.

As late as the mid-1980s, there was no account planning function within U.S. advertising agencies. Now, the trade association for the U.S. advertising community, the American Association of Advertising Agencies (AAAA), holds annual conferences for account planning that attract hundreds of attendees. The AAAA's Jay Chiat Planning Awards attract hundreds of entries each year. Account planning certainly has come of age and is a mainstay in the advertising community.

Changing the Fundamentals of the Agency Structure

The origins of advertising account planning rest with two advertising agencies that saw the need for someone to bridge the gaps between client, agency, and consumer. What may be construed as an elevated research function performed by people who excel at interpreting research and making it useful has developed into a method or process that makes advertising more effective.

For many agencies, advertising account planning is the fourth pillar of agency function. The other three are account management, creative, and media. Agencies that have adopted account planning see it as a different skill set, separate from account management or research but spanning both areas. Traditionally, account managers manage the client/agency relationship and counsel the client. Researchers are more often concerned with using the right research technique to fit the problem and are heavily weighted toward quantitative research. The account planner fills gaps or voids in this process by synthesizing consumer information that must be thoroughly considered in the application of marketing and advertising strategy and execution.

The fundamental change of inserting an account planner into the advertising process as an equal to account management, creative, and media has had a profound effect on each area. For the account managers, it has meant giving up some control of the advertising process. Where the account manager would once dominate advertising strategy, now the account planner has a significant say in the matter. It means that the creative group will influence the message development throughout the creative process. The creative pro-

Figure 1.2 **New Way of Structuring Agency/Client Relationship**

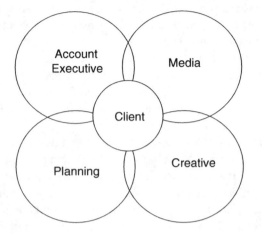

cess now has ongoing consumer critiques where before it only had to pass muster with the client and the account manager. For the media group, it has meant that selecting media is not just about cost efficiencies. The account planner adds another dimension to the media planning process. Figure 1.2 shows the new structure of an agency/client relationship.

This shift to account planning has not always gone smoothly. Few people are willing to concede control of their work. Yet that is what the account planner is asking each department or discipline to do. Obviously, this shift in power has had its share of skeptics and critics within the agency community. This has led to a difference in the account planning role, depending upon the agency's philosophy and culture.

What an Account Planner Does

What an account planner does varies from agency to agency. An account planner can have a focused role in the advertising process or a more generalist role in the full spectrum of marketing and communications strategy.

In the broadest sense, the account planner represents the consumer point of view in the marketing and advertising process. Much as an actor understands his character, the account planner immerses himself or herself in the consumer mind-set at every phase of the brand purchase cycle. As a result, the account planner can add value to a wide variety of business and advertising areas. Thus the description of an account planner's work can range from business strategy to advertising strategy down to specific creative content and media contact strategy briefs.

In the narrowest definition, the advertising account planner is a part of the advertising creative process. In this case, the product that the account planner produces is the creative brief, which is the basis of various forms of message content produced by the creative group.

While advertising account planners certainly know a lot about research and use research in their jobs, they are very different from traditional market researchers. A market researcher finds out about a consumer through various research methodologies. An account planner takes it a step further and identifies with the consumer, internalizing the research. A market researcher can show you statistics about how consumers behave. An account planner should be able to tell you not only who your customers are but what they feel.

From an advertising viewpoint, the account planner should insert the consumer's viewpoint all along the path of advertising strategy and creation. This differs from the role of the market researcher, who tests ideas after the creative work is completed. This is one of the fundamental reasons why account planning took hold in the United Kingdom and continues to gain traction around the world today. The account planning process engages the consumer and aids the agency in understanding the consumers' emotions.

Depending on the organization, an account planner can be an advertising strategist, a business consultant, a consumer ombudsman for the creative and/ or media group, or merely a creative brief producer. It all depends upon the commitment that the organization may or may not have to account planning. In this book, we view the role of the account planner as a complete advertising strategist who impacts all aspects of the advertising process.

Impact of Account Planning

There are still people within the advertising community who wonder what the big deal is about account planning. Advertising has always been planned and campaigns have always been measured in some manner. So some may ask: Aren't we doing this activity anyway? Do we really need a separate department or function for this activity? Isn't the advertising account planner really just a glorified qualitative researcher? What exactly is the return on investment for adding an account planner to the staff?

All are valid questions that have been debated within the advertising community as well as by outside interests. However, the advent of account planning has come at a time when the advertising industry needs it. The rise of the information age has greatly increased the need for account planning within an agency. As consumer information became more pervasive and reliable, marketers were much more able to understand the behavior of consumers regarding their brand. However, with all the information available in today's marketplace, there becomes an even greater need for insight. Turning information into insights about consumers is the essence of being a good account planner.

Another area where account planning is making its mark within other countries is due to the marketplace itself. The United States and many European countries are mature marketplaces for many goods and services. This has led to an increasing difficulty in differentiating one's brand or service based on a unique product attribute. This maturation of the market means that brand differentiation is much more likely to come through an emotional benefit rather than a unique product attribute or functional benefit. Helping guide marketers through the emotional maze is one of the hallmarks of account planning.

The explosion of media choices, the rise of digital media and conversational marketing, and an increasingly fragmented marketplace have led to a need for more complex brand contact strategies. No longer do cost efficiencies alone drive media programs in today's marketplace. The goal of communications planning is to understand how the consumer engages with media and the brand. Understanding the consumer reflects strength in account planning.

For the advertising community, the account planner is one of the keys to swinging the pendulum back in favor of agencies as thought leaders in consumer insight. Account planners are leading the charge to uncover insights from the morass of marketing information that is available today. They impact every aspect of the marketing communications process.

Advertising account planning can be a job, a process, or a way of approaching business planning. Regardless of what it is in an organization, it should become the mind-set for all those involved in an integrated marketing communications campaign. Advertising account planning is about keeping the consumer at the center of the marketing and communications universe. That is why account planning has become a true force in communications planning.

Review Questions

1. How does advertising account planning differ from market research?
2. How does account planning differ from account management?
3. How does account planning bring the various marketing and advertising functions together?
4. How has account planning changed the role of the advertising agency in the client relationship?

Discussion Questions

1. What is meant by the differences between qualitative and quantitative research? Give some examples.
2. How can an account planner work effectively with so many different communications functions?
3. Why does account planning impact all levels of the integrated marketing communications process rather than at just a single level?
4. How does the job description of the account planner differ from other roles in the agency?

Additional Resources

Many of these sources will be useful throughout this book.

Cooper, Alan. *How to Plan Advertising.* London: Cassell, 1997.

Hackley, C. "Account Planning: Current Agency Perspective on an Advertising Enigma." *Journal of Advertising Research* 43 (2) (June 2003): 235–45.

Kessler, S. *Chiat/Day.* New York: Rizzoli, 1990.

Lannon, J., and M. Baskin. *A Master Class in Brand Planning: The Timeless Works of Stephen King.* Hoboken, NJ: Wiley, 2007.

Pollitt, S. *Pollitt on Planning.* London: Admap Publications, 2008.

Reis, A., and J. Trout. *Positioning: The Battle for Your Mind.* New York: McGraw-Hill, 2001.

Samuel, L. *The Trend Commandments: Turning Cultural Fluency into Marketing Opportunity.* New York: Bang! Zoom! Books, 2003.

Stabiner, K. *Inventing Desire. Inside Chiat/Day: The Hottest Shop, the Coolest Players, the Big Business of Advertising.* New York: Simon & Schuster, 1993.

Steel, J. *Truth, Lies and Advertising: The Art of Account Planning.* New York: Wiley, 1998.

Weichselbaum, H., and A. Hardy. *Readings in Account Planning.* Chicago: Copy Workshop, 2006.

Chapter 2

The Role That Account Planning
Plays in a Campaign

Account planning can play a role in virtually every phase of the integrated marketing communications process. While some agencies choose to limit the account planning role to creative development, others offer a more expanded view. With the integration of account planning at media, public relations, and digital companies, one way or another account planning or the principles of account planning are being woven into various facets of campaigns.

As we mentioned previously, our point of view is that account planning can and should play a role in every aspect of an integrated campaign. That raises the question of what goes into a complete integrated marketing communications campaign. To answer that question, we reviewed hundreds of case studies from both the professional and academic sectors. Since marketing and advertising campaigns and their playbooks are proprietary, we sought the published case studies from the Effie Awards, IPA Effectiveness Awards, Jay Chiat Planning Awards, and the American Advertising Federation (AAF)-National Student Advertising Competition (NSAC) award winners to act as proxies for what makes up a campaign.

The Effie Awards and IPA Effectiveness Awards are cut from the same cloth. Both focus on the effectiveness of communications. To win either an Effie or an IPA Effectiveness Award, the campaign must contribute to some metric of moving the brand forward. This involves both market and mind metrics. From a market standpoint, the goal to be measured may be building sales, increasing brand penetration and/or frequency of purchase, among others. And from a mind standpoint, the goal may be to change a perception, increase awareness, get the brand into the considered set, and add to its quality perception, among other metrics. The campaign must prove results and the judges must consider the problem to be difficult to overcome; so much so that the strategy and results are surprising.

Where the Effie Awards and IPA Effectiveness Awards differ is in structure and intent. The IPA Effectiveness Awards, based in London, are associated with the World Advertising Research Council (WARC). The core purpose of the IPA Effectiveness Awards is to demonstrate the financial payback for investment in marketing communications. Each year, the winners are added to the IPA databank of cases that provides a tremendous research resource on how communications work. As a result, the IPA Effectiveness awards are more rigorous in terms of identifying the specific communications impact on the brand's finances than the Effies are. And the IPA Effectiveness Awards are all written in a very similar format so that they can be catalogued and analyzed for future research. This is not a knock on the Effies, which is a very prestigious award and draws more worldwide competition than the IPA Effectiveness Awards. It is that the IPA Effectiveness Awards are a much richer resource in the study of advertising.

The AAAA Jay Chiat Planning Award is the only industry award that focuses on account planning. In 2002, the AAAA, the U.S. trade association, inherited the Account Planning Group-U.S. Account Planning Awards and renamed them the AAAA Jay Chiat Awards as a tribute to the man who brought account planning to the United States. While the criterion for these awards is to create campaigns that have an impact on the market, the focus is more on the strategies of thinking and creative message formulation. The key criterion for winning this award is to link a great strategic idea with an equally impactful creative expression of that idea.

The AAF-NSAC competition is the only national collegiate advertising competition in the United States. Every year, hundreds of colleges and universities compete through the AAF to win the account. Each school has the same client brief or case study and must develop a thirty-two-page plan book covering all aspects of an integrated marketing communications plan and then deliver a twenty-minute presentation of the plan to judges in each of the fifteen AAF districts. It is probably the largest new business pitch in the advertising industry. Obviously, beyond the difference between student and professional work, the AAF-NSAC is about what you plan to do compared to the industry awards, which are about what you have done.

From these award-winning plans we can spot some clear patterns in how campaigns are organized, the judging of what makes an award-winning effort, and how account planning plays a role in the process. Let's first review the outline or structure that is included in a campaign.

Campaign Contents

To review the content of a campaign, we will review the IPA Effectiveness Awards and the AAF-NSAC student competition awards. There is something

Figure 2.1 **Effectiveness Awards: Case Study Outline**

1. Introduction
2. Background
3. Statement of problem
4. Role of communications
5. Communications strategy/idea
6. Creative solution
7. Media solution
8. Communication measurement results
9. Business measurement results
10. Return on investment

Figure 2.2 **NSAC Campaign Outline**

1. Executive summary
2. Situation analysis
3. Primary research plan and results/brand positioning
4. Target segmentation analysis
5. Creative objectives/strategies
6. Big idea
7. Creative executions
8. Contact plan: Traditional, nontraditional, digital, promotions, and public relations
9. Campaign evaluation and return on investment

to be learned from both the professional and student sides of the equation. The IPA Effectiveness Awards are consistent in their case study approach and while the AAF-NSAC plan books vary in approach, there is a strong pattern of success throughout the years by the winning teams. The outline in this book is a composite of the winning plan books from the past ten years.

Figures 2.1 and 2.2 provide outlines for the IPA Effectiveness Awards and the AAF-NSAC plan books. There are some similarities and some differences in what is covered. We will review the major sections of the plans. The key to a well-written plan includes the following:

- Put the plan in context for the reader.
- Establish the situation.
- Define the target market.
- Identify the problem.
- Identify the strategy to solve the problem.
- Discuss how that insight is executed creatively.
- Discuss how that insight is executed in communication channels.
- Discuss the results or how you plan to measure the results.

These are the fundamental building blocks for organizing a successful campaign plan. It is up to the author then to tell the story in a fun and interesting manner. Let's discuss each of the key sections.

Putting the Plan in Context

All of the campaign case studies or plan books have a similar start. Each uses an introduction or executive summary to tell the story of the campaign. The role of the account planner is to set the story that establishes the context for what the readers will see as they plow through the case study or plan book. It also sums up, in four or five short paragraphs, what the problem was and how it was solved.

For example, here are the opening sentences for the introduction to the 2008 Gold Award–winning IPA Effectiveness Award winner, written by Ed Booty and Jude Lowson of BBH in London. The campaign was for KFC in Europe:

> This is the story of a dramatic revival in the fortune of one of the nation's best-known fast food brands. It is a revival against all odds, and a revival achieved by going against every received wisdom in the category.

As you can see, this is very compelling copy. It makes you want to see how they solved this dilemma. For the AAF-NSAC plans, putting the plan in context is like an executive summary of what you plan to do. Unlike the IPA or other industry awards, the AAF-NSAC competition is about what you plan to do rather than what you have accomplished. However, it still should be written in a compelling manner since that is the first thing that a judge will see when reviewing the plan book.

Establish the Situation

The situation or background paints the picture of what the brand is facing. The situation covers a number of key elements. The role of the account planner is to synthesize the information and to make the situation into a compelling story. One easy way to organize your thoughts in the situation analysis is to think of the three Cs: Company, Competition, and the Consumer. The first is a review of the company and the brand itself. This may contain elements such as the company history, its size and scope, its assets, and any brand elements that it has previously featured.

There should also be a section devoted to the market and market conditions. For example, if you were working on KFC, as in the example above, you would want to understand the breadth and depth of the fast food industry as well as any trends that might impact it. This could be a rise in healthy eating or a demographic trend, such as fewer young adults that can feed the category. It should also include how the industry is segmented. This can be by type of business or by the benefits that the business or brand delivers.

Another aspect of the situation analysis or background that is tied into the market and market conditions is an analysis of the competition. Identifying who the competitors are and their specific strengths and weaknesses is a crucial aspect of determining the situation.

The other aspect of the situation analysis is a review of the consumer from a demographic and a psychographic perspective. This will include secondary and primary research regarding the consumers, their needs, and how your brand meets these needs within this competitive framework.

Define the Target Market

One aspect that typically comes out of the research developed in the situation analysis is a segmentation of the target audience. This segmentation will generate the platform and insights to help develop the campaign. Obviously, determining the target market is a key component to the success of any communications campaign. Whether working on the goals demographic, psychographic, or behavioral, the role of the account planner is to ensure that the target market opportunity should be quantified in terms of how it can meet the overall marketing objectives, as well as how it can be influenced from a communications perspective.

Painting a picture of the target market is crucial to brand positioning as well as creative and media development. A good example of painting a picture of a target audience is in the 2008 AAF-NSAC award-winning campaign plan by students at Ohio University. Here is how they described the target for the America Online's Instant Messenger product.

"The target audience is 18–24 year old males and females, who we refer to as Constant Connectors. These individuals are hyper-active, trendy, tech-savvy, and dependent on fast and easy communication."

The segmentation in this case is an eighteen to twenty-four-year-old age group, which is further refined by how they choose to communicate. In every case study, whether it is from the industry or from the student competition, developing a cohesive target market is the bedrock of any good campaign.

Identify the Problem

While identifying the problem may sound simple, it can actually be quite difficult. That is why the IPA Effectiveness Awards requires a state-ment of the problem and the role that communications play in solving the problem. This is a crucial area for account planners since they are largely responsible for stating the consumer problem and linking it to the business problem.

For example, suppose that you are working on an orange juice account where sales are down 10 percent. This could be the result of a myriad of items. The weather may have been exceedingly bad that year, which impacted the ability to generate product. Or a key chain of grocery stores may have elected to not carry the brand. Or there was a bumper crop of oranges, which depressed the prices. Or there was negative publicity surrounding the use of pesticides in growing the crop. These are all valid reasons for why sales are down 10 percent, but there is little that advertising can do to change it.

Advertising and all of communications need a *consumer* problem to solve. Identifying a consumer problem is paramount in the process. Matching that problem to the overall business problem is crucial in linking the two outcomes: the goals for both the consumer groups and for the business. All of this leads to properly defining the role that communications will play in solving the problem.

In the orange juice case, a problem that communications could solve would be to increase the nutritional value of the brand to increase penetration among young mothers.

Identify the Strategy That Solves the Problem

Once a problem has been identified, it is time for a solution. Solving a communications problem is based on uncovering a consumer insight that leads to a "big idea." This is the bastion of account planning. An insight can come from considering an entire category, thinking about the competitive situation or from observing the consumer. Regardless of where it comes from, the insight is the underpinning to the overarching idea.

The big idea is sometimes called a strategic idea or just a communications strategy. Regardless, the idea is the single-minded proposition that drives the communications forward.

A good example of this is found in the 2006 Jay Chiat Planning Awards Global Gold award winner, submitted by McCann-Erickson. The campaign was for MasterCard. The team's consumer insight was that "consumers were moving away from living the high life to living a 'my-life.'" It is a change from outward to inward expression of wealth. This insight led to the strategic idea "MasterCard is the best way to pay for everything that matters."

We all know the "Priceless" campaign that resulted from this insight and strategic idea. Setting the idea into motion by uncovering consumer insights is the consummate role of the account planner.

Creative and Media Execution of the Strategy

Everyone remembers the MasterCard "Priceless" campaign. It is one of the classic advertising campaigns of our age. When you understand the strategy behind it, it becomes more evident why it resonates so well with the consumer. One of the key roles of account planning is to ensure that strategy meets execution. You can have a great strategy poorly executed or a poor strategy with a great execution. Neither will be effective in the marketplace.

The role of the account planner is to make sure that the creative and media solutions are in concert with the strategy as well as with each other. In today's fragmented media world, how you execute the strategy is increasingly more challenging. It also means that you need a big idea that can cross over a variety of paid and nonpaid channels of communication.

All of the award cases have similar presentations of creative elements. They all highlight the key aspects of the program whether via television and print or digital and guerilla advertising.

Where the student competition differs from the industry is in the devotion to an integrated plan that contains a wide variety of media, promotions, and public relations. In this book, all of these elements are covered in detail in the student case studies while media are typically just highlighted in the industry case studies. The exception to this is industry media planning awards.

The account planner helps the creative group by keeping them on strategy and adding consumer voice to continually evaluate the work. The account planner helps the media team by assisting in showing them where the brand and the consumer interact. This can lead to interesting and engaging media planning strategies that cross all media channels.

Measurement of Results

The last stage of a campaign is how it performed in the marketplace. This involves measuring the business performance as well as the communication performance. The role of the account planner is to work with the client and agency team on setting the appropriate metrics and tying communication performance to business results.

Measurement is where the student competition differs from the industry. The industry awards are based on actual performance whereas the student competition is based on estimated performance. The similarities between the industry and the student competitions are that they both require a detailed plan on how to measure results.

The IPA Effectiveness Awards provide the most rigorous examples of

Figure 2.3   AAF National Student Advertising Competition: Plan Book Composite Score Sheet

1. Creative Strategies (35 percent of plan book score)
   - Presents an elegant and easy-to-understand creative approach.
   - Clearly shows the link between the research and creative approach.
   - Emphasizes creative ideas and thinking that utilize both traditional and nontraditional marketing elements.
   - Uses innovative thinking to reach the goals of the campaign.

2. Positioning, Targeting, and Research (25 percent of plan book score)
   - Effective use of primary and secondary research.
   - Develops strategic positioning for the brand that is derived from research.
   - Provides a target audience recommendation that is derived from research.
   - Effectively covers the demographics and psychographics of the target.
   - Recommends effective campaign evaluation methods.

3. Media Strategy (15 percent of plan book score)
   - Effective, efficient, and creative use of media.
   - Develops a mix of traditional and nontraditional media.
   - Understands the needs for market segmentation and how to effectively reach those markets.
   - Effectively uses research to link target audience to media vehicles.

4. Integration of Communications Tools (15 percent of plan book score)
   - Creates a cohesive marketing communications plan. (Do all the pieces work together?)
   - Demonstrates an effective blending of advertising, publicity, public relations, promotions, and other tools as needed.
   - Demonstrates an effective phasing on when and how to apply each communication tool.
   - Shows forward thinking on why and how the plan could be adjusted in the future.

5. General Quality of the Plan Book (10 percent of plan book score)
   - Professional appearance/ability to serve as a selling tool: logical and clear writing.
   - Free of grammatical, spelling, and syntax errors.
   - Creative approach to delivering both the information and recommendations.

measurement. As Figure 2.1 shows, the IPA cases offer specific results for communication measures such as awareness or perception change, and business measures such as sales, switching behavior, or other marketing or business metrics.

Where the IPA differs from other case studies is not only the rigor of providing a series of metrics but in isolating the contribution of communication to the business results. While other cases may provide business results, the IPA cases actually work to eliminate any variable outside of communication that could have contributed to the results. Thereby, the IPA cases provide a pure communications return on investment; meaning that they specifically

Figure 2.4   **Jay Chiat Account-Planning Awards: Criteria for Judging Effectiveness**

Judges were asked to evaluate planning excellence based on the following definitions:

- Brilliant strategic thinking.
- Is this a previously unearthed insight?
- Is there new thinking in the role of communications?
- Is there new thinking in media or channels?
- Was new ground broken in measurement?
- Did this expand the frontiers of the discipline?
- Powerful creative expression of the idea.
- Is there a clear link between the thinking and the creative?
- Do you believe this creative would have happened without planning?
- Is there new thinking in the execution of the idea?
- Is this great creative?
- Did this work have an impact, either in the market or in some other measure?

tell the reader that a dollar spent on communication generated X dollars in incremental revenue. Given the complexities of proving return on investment (ROI), this type of rigorous analysis is an invaluable tool both for the marketer and the agency to prove the value of their specific integrated marketing communications program.

Campaign Criteria for Effectiveness

We know that campaigns are judged to be effective by their return on investment. That is a given. But an award-winning campaign does much more than simply produce good business results. It is the result of a well-crafted case study that has a great strategic idea, impactful creative and surprising media, and a clear link between strategy and execution.

Figure 2.3 shows a compilation of the AAF-NSAC plan book score sheet. This is how students are "graded" in their plan development. Compare this to the Account Planning Awards for the advertising industry, as seen in Figure 2.4. While there are some differences, the criteria for judging an award-winning campaign are quite similar. The scoring demonstrates the importance of account planning or account planning principles in a full campaign.

One of the key aspects to both student and industry judging criteria is the need to first present a brilliant strategy or an elegant approach to the problem. From this strategy, it is imperative that there is a clear link between the idea and the creative expression of the idea. These are key aspects of winning either competition.

Both also have a quest for using research in new and unusual ways. Judges are looking for new insights or new methods of using research to uncover those insights. The fundamentals include developing a clear position for the brand and a strong target segmentation. The separation between the fundamentals and a winning program is the ability to push the limits into new areas. This includes all facets of the campaign from the big idea to the media or contact plan. All of it must be cohesive and fit together with no disparate parts.

In summary, account planning plays a role in every aspect of a campaign regardless of whether you are a professional or a student. The greater the insight, the greater need there is for the account planner or others who are applying account planning principles. As you read each of the subsequent chapters, we will describe the role of the account planner and how to tackle each facet of an integrated marketing communications campaign.

Review Questions

1. What are the key components of an integrated marketing communications campaign?
2. What are the differences and similarities in how professionals and students develop award-winning campaign case studies?
3. What do judges look for in award-winning case studies?

Discussion Questions

1. What are other outlines or components of an advertising campaign? Have the aspects of a campaign changed over time?
2. Should student campaigns mirror that of the industry or should they follow a different pattern?
3. Is there a better way to make the judging of awards less subjective?

Additional Resources

Kim, W.C., and R. Mauborgne. *Blue Ocean Strategy: How to Create Uncontested Market Space and Make Competition Irrelevant.* Hoboken, NJ: Wiley, 2005.
Steel, J. *Truth, Lies and Advertising: The Art of Account Planning.* Hoboken, NJ: Wiley, 1998.

Chapter 3
Brand Destination Planning

There are many moving pieces and parts involved in developing an award-winning campaign. Getting every aspect of your marketing communications aligned is a real challenge. Just like embarking on any journey, developing a brand requires a roadmap to see where it begins and where it's headed. This roadmap may be called a brand plan, a brand vision, or, as in this book, brand destination planning.

Unlike a road trip, where you are in one place and need to go to another, a brand never stands still. It is constantly in motion. There are outside forces that help shape it. There are inside forces that help guide it. A key role for the account planner is to work with the brand team to define where they want to go. Determining the destination or vision for the brand is an important first step in developing a campaign.

Many times you see communication that may reflect a short-term initiative such as generating sales this weekend or responding to a public relations crisis. If a brand or company only responds to short-term pressures, there will be no long-term value in its communications. There is always a destination that is the most desirable place for the brand. You want all communication efforts to lead there and not get stuck on a side road. You always want to add value to the brand regardless of what marketing lever you are pushing. The only way to establish a forward-thinking strategy is to provide a roadmap that leads to the appropriate destination.

The Brand Destination Process

Brand planning leads into campaign planning. You can't develop one without the other. The brand destination process is one method that helps put everyone on the same page. Brand destination planning is based on answering some fundamental questions about the brand, such as

Figure 3.1   **Brand Destination Process**

- Where are we today?
- Where do we want to be?
- What is in the way of getting there?
- How can we get there?
- Are we getting there?

These answers to these questions are the foundation to all the details that go into developing a successful campaign. Figure 3.1 provides a schematic of what the brand destination process is all about. Let's take a look at the framework behind each question.

To answer the first question, "Where are we today?" you need to know the history of the brand, its strengths and weaknesses, how consumers perceive it, who buys it, and why they buy it. With this information you can begin to paint a picture of where the brand has been, where it is today, and where it looks like it is going.

To answer this question requires research. Figure 3.1 provides a summary of all the research that culminates in an answer to the initial question. You want to learn what consumers current believe or think about the brand. Do they think it is of high quality or is it the low-price leader? Is it cool or is it dated? Is it just like every other brand in the category or does it stand out? This is the type of information that goes into the top box in the diagram.

The other aspect of this question lies in understanding consumer behavior.

Figure 3.2   **Brand Destination Process: The Tide Detergent Example**

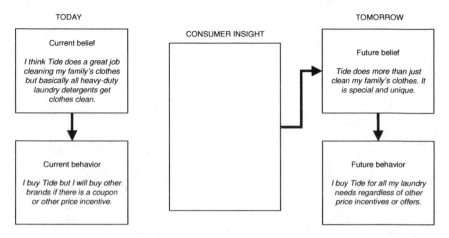

Do consumers purchase your brand exclusively or do they rotate among a set of brands? Do they buy your brand just when it is on sale or do they buy your brand in the face of competitive discounting? This information about purchase behavior can be used to answer the initial question.

Together this paints a picture of the combination of factors that have impacted our position in the marketplace. The brand destination summarizes where we are today. It is also important to know how this position has changed over time. These changes will impact where you can take the brand.

Today Versus Tomorrow Viewpoint

The second question is, "Where do we want to be?" What do we want consumers to think of us and how do we want to change that behavior? This is a judgmental exercise. For example, it would likely be impossible for McDonald's to convince consumers that it offered more exclusive service than a premier five-star restaurant. However, it might not be a leap to say that McDonald's could be seen as an alternative to a casual dining restaurant. In creating a vision for the future of a brand you must balance hopes and dreams with reality.

Let's take Tide laundry detergent as an example of a brand that changed its campaign and position in the market. Figure 3.2 illustrates the brand destination process. In this case, a mom with kids is the consumer. Mom's initial belief of Tide was that it did get her family's clothes clean; even the very difficult dirty ones. But, she didn't see a big enough difference between

Tide and other brands to only buy Tide. She would buy other brands if there were incentives such as lower prices or coupons.

The future vision for the brand was one where Tide was seen as a unique laundry detergent that met Mom's family needs all the time. If Mom believed that Tide did more than just clean her clothes, she would then buy the product regardless of competitive incentives.

Crafting a vision for the future starts with a basic premise but requires insight to complete it. It also requires reviewing the future vision to ensure that it is unique in the market. In Tide's case, they wanted to develop a position where they were known for more than just deep cleaning. Tide understood that just deep cleaning wasn't unique so they needed to determine what was.

Barriers to Reaching Tomorrow

There are always barriers to achieving tomorrow's vision. Barriers can be consumer perceptions. They can be consumer priorities or values. They can be competitive threats. They can be outside influences such as the economy or legislation. This is the point at which you should recap anything, whether internal or external, that you believe is standing in the way of achieving this new vision or goal.

In essence this is developing the situation analysis. Chapter 4 focuses on a complete detailing of what goes into a situation analysis. Obviously, a good exercise to conduct within the situation analysis that helps surface barriers is the SWOT (strengths, weaknesses, opportunities, and threats) analysis. SWOT analysis is a great tool for crafting vision as well as determining barriers that might stand in the way of attaining it.

In our Tide example, here is how the brand assessed some of the key barriers to reaching their goal. From a consumer perspective, a mom with a large family is on a very tight budget. She is constantly looking for ways to save money. Money pressures force her to weigh every purchase decision. She may give up a bit of quality to save some money that can be used elsewhere to support the family. As a result, this consumer is an active coupon seeker. She is always looking for deals. So, being able to stretch her budget is crucial.

This consumer views Tide as the clear leader in the category and a brand that will get the really dirty clothes clean. This is a benefit, particularly if the mom has young boys who get their clothes very dirty. However, Mom views all laundry detergents as having the ability to get clothes clean. So, while Tide may get them slightly cleaner, she can still get them adequately clean with other brands. Essentially, mom doesn't believe that Tide may be worth the extra dollars required to buy the brand over others.

Just to add more gravity to the consumer mind-set, the U.S. economy at the time was in a tailspin, so there was even more pressure on consumers to save their money. To add more competitive pressure to Tide's position, the retailers' private label brands had also gained strength. Tide had to overcome both consumer and competitive barriers to achieve its vision.

Developing Insight to Break Through the Barriers

To bust through these barriers requires some serious thought. It involves gaining some form of insight that will lead to a compelling story that will change the perception of the brand in the marketplace. This is when you need to answer the next question, "How can we get there?"

The challenge to answering this question is to match a compelling future vision with an equally compelling way to get there. In doing this, you need to consider whether the goal is attainable. This involves reflection on why you may not have reached the goal in the past. And you need to consider whether your competition has been successful in attaining the same goal. Finally, you need develop enough rational supporting evidence so that a consumer will believe this new vision.

This is hard stuff. It requires a lot of soul-searching and a lot of consumer research. To work through this phase requires gaining new insight or acting on something you already know.

Let's take a look at how Tide tackled their problem. Tide knew that just getting clothes clean wasn't enough for Mom. Tide also wouldn't lower its price to compete with other less expensive alternatives. So, they were trapped. They were unable to come up with a formula that got clothes any cleaner and they couldn't lower the price. What *could* they do? They needed to find something more important to Mom than just cleaning clothes. And that is what they did.

Through consumer research, Tide found that mom was more concerned about her children's clothes wearing out than keeping them clean. Because she of her tight budget, she couldn't afford to buy new clothes all the time. And washing clothes frequently contributes to wearing them out. So the trade-off was between higher price and less frequent shopping and not between brands. She would save the difference between buying Tide and another brand to help fund more clothes for the kids. So Tide decided to convince Mom that washing with Tide would extend the life of her children's clothes.

Figure 3.3 shows how Tide incorporated this consumer insight into building a future belief that would reinforce the desired future behavior. In Tide's case, this insight was the idea that drove Tide to change their conversation from cleaning clothes to making them last longer. While Tide still has an advantage in deep cleaning, it has pushed to a new advantage in helping Mom manage her budget by keeping her children's clothes looking new and lasting longer.

Figure 3.4 recaps the entire brand destination process using Tide as an example. Just like any case, it all looks so simple when it is explained. All you have to do is find an insight, right? While it does take experience to find insights that lead to big ideas there are methods to make it easier.

Generating Insights

You know that you have found an insight if any of the following happens:

- You think, "Aha! It was there all along."
- You think, "Duh. Anyone could see that."
- Your competitor thinks, "Oh no! They are doing something unexpected."
- The consumer thinks, "Ah . . . this brand really understands me."

Insights are usually obvious once they are in sight but when used they can disrupt a category. That is the elegance and power behind finding compelling insights. Account planners look for "quality-of-life" insights. Basically, this means asking, "How does this insight make my life (target audience) better?" So, in the Tide case, the insight was that Mom was concerned about clothes wearing out. If Tide could make clothes last longer, that would add to the quality of her life.

The following are some key places to look for insights that will drive the idea behind a campaign.

- Perceiving a difference in the product or brand that intersects with the quality of life.
- Overcoming a perceived barrier in the mind of the consumer regarding your brand.
- Finding untapped consumer beliefs that the category is not addressing.
- Finding associations that enhance how the consumers see themselves.

Finding insights is always a tough job. It is even more difficult to teach. It all comes down to learning how to read the consumer and the brand's situation. Studying award-winning cases is one way to get into the mind-set of account planners to learn how they approach a problem.

Figure 3.3 **Brand Destination Process: The Tide Detergent Example**

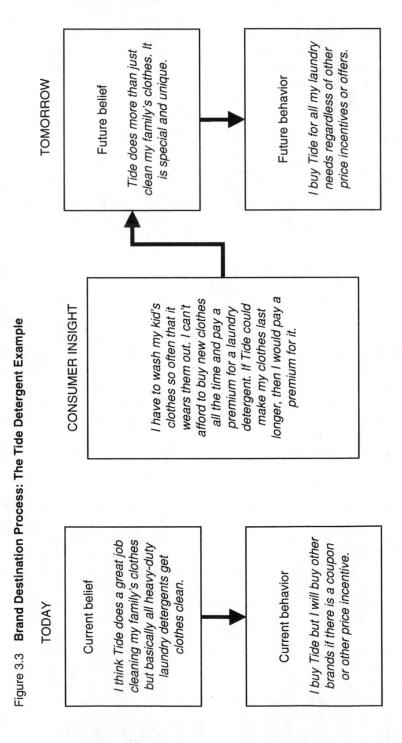

TODAY

Current belief

I think Tide does a great job cleaning my family's clothes but basically all heavy-duty laundry detergents get clothes clean.

Current behavior

I buy Tide but I will buy other brands if there is a coupon or other price incentive.

CONSUMER INSIGHT

I have to wash my kid's clothes so often that it wears them out. I can't afford to buy new clothes all the time and pay a premium for a laundry detergent. If Tide could make my clothes last longer, then I would pay a premium for it.

TOMORROW

Future belief

Tide does more than just clean my family's clothes. It is special and unique.

Future behavior

I buy Tide for all my laundry needs regardless of other price incentives or offers.

Figure 3.4 **Brand Destination Process: The Tide Detergent Example**

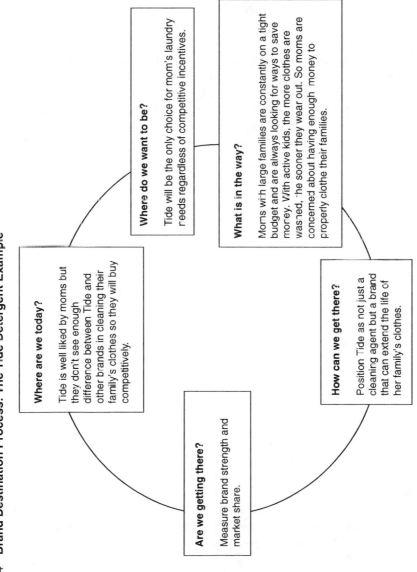

Where do we want to be?

Tide will be the only choice for mom's laundry needs regardless of competitive incentives.

What is in the way?

Moms with large families are constantly on a tight budget and are always looking for ways to save money. With active kids, the more clothes are washed, the sooner they wear out. So moms are concerned about having enough money to properly clothe their families.

Where are we today?

Tide is well liked by moms but they don't see enough difference between Tide and other brands in cleaning their family's clothes so they will buy competitively.

Are we getting there?

Measure brand strength and market share.

How can we get there?

Position Tide as not just a cleaning agent but a brand that can extend the life of her family's clothes.

For example, the Bahamas Tourism case provides an interesting example of finding an untapped consumer belief that the category wasn't addressing. Travel destinations such as the Bahamas have long touted their specific attributes as the best places to take a vacation. The Bahamas have great beaches, plenty of fun in the sun recreation, and the ability to gamble if you so choose. But just about any Caribbean island can claim the same thing.

In this case, the Fallon agency began to look at the trends among people taking vacations. They found that compared to other developed countries, Americans receive the fewest vacation days. Even so, Americans still leave at least four days of unclaimed vacation each year. This led Fallon to take a step back and assess where travel destinations fell in the consumer's mind. The insight was to address *why* a person would want to go on vacation, rather than *where* they would want to go. The quality of life insight was simply, "You need a vacation." The creative leap from this insight was to "take a Bahamavention." Fallon positioned the Bahamas as a destination for the vacation deprived rather than just another pretty beach.

A current example of tapping into how consumers see themselves is evidenced in the award-winning campaign for Dove. Ogilvy & Mather is the worldwide representative for Dove products. The problem facing Dove was that their advertising was just like everyone else's in the category. It was based on achieving a specific beauty ideal that was unattainable for a wide majority of women. Yet the conventional wisdom in the beauty category was to associate your brand with someone who was beautiful: usually a model or a famous film star. The problem was that the category boiled down to which company had the trendiest model or the most popular film star.

The insight that Ogilvy brought to the brand was that while the beauty category was all about product personalization, everyone in the ads looked alike. This led to an aha moment: Why do women have to look a certain way to be beautiful? Research found that only 2 percent of women in the United States saw themselves as beautiful yet 30 percent saw themselves as "natural." This led to the quality-of-life insight, "You are naturally beautiful."

Dove took this a step further and created what they term the "Big Ideal," their platform for all communication: "Dove believes that the world would be a better place if we could make more women feel more beautiful every day." This beauty manifesto was borne out by research that revealed that after reading women's magazines, 72 percent of women felt worse about themselves. This confirmed that the category advertising was actually making women feel less attractive even though it was intended to be aspirational.

The Dove campaign was built on the simple premise that there is no single standard for beauty. It seems obvious when you read the case study, yet no one in the beauty category had done it. That is the definition of a compelling insight. It is simple. It seems very obvious. Yet no one is acting on it.

Insights are the foundation of a compelling message that will move the brand toward the ultimate goal or vision. Coming up with insights is not easy, but usually the best ones are right in front of you. We will discuss linking insights to creative ideas later in this book. At this stage, it is important to understand that finding how to achieve the brand vision is not just through great creative messages. It is through great strategy that links to great creative.

The final question is, "Are we getting there? This is the measurement of progress toward the vision. Measurement issues become more self-evident as you go through the brand destination process. Identifying barriers can help determine the starting point. A benchmark study to determine where the brand stands today is a standard part of the process. From here, you can begin to measure the progress toward the goal.

In summary, the brand destination process forms the framework for campaign planning It is the brand roadmap to success. By following this simple process, you will be able to link a strategy to a measurable goal and to a creative execution. With a clear brand vision, all forms of communication become much more powerful and interconnected.

Review Questions

1. What is the brand destination process?
2. How does the brand destination process differ from a marketing plan?
3. How does the brand destination process impact advertising development?

Discussion Questions

1. Who should set the brand vision? Should it be the CEO, the Chief Marketing Officer (CMO), or the agency?
2. How does a brand vision change over time? When should it be updated?
3. How do different advertising campaigns meet the brand vision?

Additional Resources

Mark, M., and C. Pearson. *The Hero and the Outlaw: Building Extraordinary Brands through the Power of Archetypes.* Berkshire, England: McGraw-Hill, 2001.
Pringle, H., and P. Field. *Brand Immortality: How Brands Can Live Long and Prosper.* London: IPA, 2009.

Chapter 4
Situation Analysis

It is impossible to determine where you need to go if you don't know where you are. The first step in account planning and any planning for that matter is to assess the current situation. In this case, you want to determine where you are and how you got here. In assessing the situation you must look at the past as well as the present.

In reviewing a company's situation, you should review the company from a business, brand, consumer, and communication perspective. Any review should assess both the external and internal forces that may impact the company or the brand.

As an account planner, you should balance the business realities of the company with the perceptual realities of the consumer's mind-set. This is where your analysis of the company may differ from just a business analysis of the brand. Your analysis will include the consumer viewpoint.

SWOT Analysis

The traditional business analysis many companies use to assess where they are is called a SWOT analysis. Whether you are developing an award-winning professional or student campaign, you are likely to undertake this type of analysis. SWOT stands for:

- Strengths
- Weaknesses
- Opportunities
- Threats

While just about every marketing plan, award-winning or not, contains a SWOT analysis, many times the authors confuse strengths with opportunities and weaknesses with threats. A good way to think about what goes into

Figure 4.1 **The SWOT Decision Matrix**

	Opportunities tomorrow	Threats tomorrow
Strengths today	Take advantage now	Defend with current strengths
Weaknesses today	Must change to take advantage	Must change to survive

a SWOT analysis is summed up in Figure 4.1. This SWOT analysis matrix clearly spells out the differences between the areas.

There are two dimensions. The first is the origin. You are making an internal assessment of the company as well as examining external influences. The second dimension is whether the attribute is helpful or harmful in achieving your brand vision. So a strength is an aspect of the company that is helpful in achieving the brand vision. Conversely, a weakness is an aspect of the company that may impede progress or be a barrier to reaching the brand vision. An opportunity is an external force that will help you toward your goal and a threat is an external or internal force that might get in your way.

SWOT analysis is more than a listing of attributes or articles you may have read. It should be a careful consideration of internal or external influences that will help you toward your goals compared to outside influences that may get in the way of your goals. One criticism of SWOT analysis is that it doesn't lead to any action. It is merely a listing of items with no direct connection to the plan. If you use the SWOT framework, it will help make your overall analysis more thoughtful and actionable.

Research That Forms a SWOT Analysis

To develop a SWOT analysis, you need to do research. A SWOT analysis contains a blend of secondary and primary research.

Secondary research involves studying information that is available to the public that can be used to understand the history of the company, or brand, and market, as well as the market share and other internal issues. If the brand is a publicly traded company, then there will be financial statements, annual reports, and other public information available. If it is a private company, then there will be trade publications or general business publications that may have published articles about the company or that cover the industry in general.

Secondary research is also a great source of information about a brand's external influences, for example, a market trend or demographic trend that may impact the brand, or a shift in consumer sentiment or economic indicators. Secondary research can also be used to understand if there is a threat to the industry or to the company itself from a new technology or a new entrant to the category.

As you review secondary research, the initial tendency is to focus on the company and the industry it competes in. That information forms a foundation for a SWOT, but you should look outside the industry to review articles on the consumer that the industry attracts, the suppliers or vendors that can have a bearing on it, the commodities that may be a part of it, or anything that can potentially influence the business.

Primary research is needed to determine what consumers think about you. While secondary research may contain studies of the industry, there is typically no substitute for conducting your own research on the brand.

In the next few chapters we will detail the type of research that is conducted to learn about what consumers think about the brand in comparison to its competitors. Primary research is the only way you can understand how aware consumers are of your brand and its advertising, how they perceive your brand compared to other brands in the category on the items that are important to them,' and the purchase dynamics of the category and the brand.

Through an intense review of secondary information and by conducting primary research to fill in the gaps, you should be on your way to developing a strong SWOT analysis.

Internal Assessment

When you review the company or brand, you want to begin by assessing the business itself, the brand strength, operations of the company and how willing management is to commit to the brand's vision. Figure 4.2 is a strategic wheel that is a helpful guide for outlining the broad areas for review in terms of strengths and weaknesses.

Usually an account planner focuses on the brand aspects of the ledger.

Figure 4.2 **Wheel of Competitive Strategy**

These include brand equity strength, pricing power, advertising uniqueness, target market and product and/or service quality. Many of these aspects of the company are both factual and perceptual. For example, two pizza delivery companies may use the same exact ingredients in their pizza yet the consumers may perceive that one is totally superior to the other. This area plus how strong the brand is, how unique the advertising is, and who is buying the brand and who isn't are pretty common factors to consider in the area of strengths and weaknesses.

But why would an account planner want to understand the financial strength, operational strength, distribution, or even management tendencies of the company? This seems like more management consulting than campaign planning, doesn't it? As an account planner, you don't need to be able to compute sophisticated cash flow analysis but you do need to understand the operations implication of the organization. In essence, you want to be sure that the organization can deliver on the brand vision. Can the operation deliver on the promise? Do they have enough money and/or resources? Is management committed to a long-term vision? All of these questions are as important as determining the consumer viewpoint of the brand. And by studying the operations of a company, often insight is gained that can be used to build a campaign. This can be particularly true when interviewing the company personnel. Often, there are insights at a certain level of management within the company that senior management may not be aware of. When a cashier at a local grocery chain recognized that the president of her store's major competition was a regular shopper, it set into motion a campaign revolving around the notion that their service was so good, even the competition liked it.

After assessing each of these areas, it is time to analyze the strengths and weaknesses of the company.

Strengths

As an account planner, you are looking for company or brand strengths that can help move the brand toward its vision. You are also looking for strengths that you can capitalize on from a campaign perspective.

In reviewing strengths and weaknesses, there are factual and perceptual categories to consider. Let's first assess the facts about the brand and company. In reviewing them, we should ask, "What facts are we looking for that would be a sign of strength?" Here are some examples that you might consider based on the wheel of competitive strategy.

Financial Strength

- The brand is growing revenue and is profitable.
- The company has a strong balance sheet.

Operational Strength

- The brand has been able to reduce costs in manufacturing the product.
- The company has a full complement of personnel.
- The company has undergone a 6 Sigma process.

Management Strength

- The management team has had a track record of growth.
- The management has invested in brand growth.
- The management participates in brand vision.

Distribution

- The brand is present in all points of distribution.
- The brand is the category captain (many retailers look to the leader of a specific category to work with on growing the category within the retailer's store).

Pricing

- The brand has been able to increase prices without losing customers.

Target Market

- The brand has been growing its market share.
- The brand has been growing its penetration.

All of these are facts that can be gathered either through secondary or primary research. If a brand has these types of strengths, then you know that you are riding a real winner. Perceptual strength is just as important as business strength. The following are some perceptual strengths to consider for a brand.

Product/Service Quality

- The brand is perceived as the best quality in its category.
- Consumers view the brand as a good value regardless of price.
- The brand has been judged as a quality winner through some form of survey, such as a J.D. Power ranking.

Brand Equity

- Consumers have a strong awareness of the brand.
- Consumers like the brand.
- Consumers believe that the brand is unique.
- Consumers first consider this brand when making a purchase choice.

Advertising

- Consumers are aware of the advertising.
- Consumers like the advertising.
- Consumers feel that the advertising is unique.
- Consumers talk about the advertising.

Psychological Equity

- The company or brand is a part of the fabric of society.
- Consumers would miss the brand or company if it went away.
- Consumers count on the brand or company to make their lives better.

As you review the strengths of a brand or company, these lists just discussed help create a checklist to consider. It is important to review the strengths of the company within the context of the competitive set. And it is important to review the strengths in terms of what they can do to move you toward your goal.

Weaknesses

As we have said, weaknesses are elements that can get in the way of attaining our goals. While you can take the above strengths and just put a "not" in the statement to make it a weakness, assessing weakness is more than just a listing. A true weakness is a barrier to achieving success. As you review a weakness, you should ask yourself how you might break through that barrier. By assessing weaknesses, you will have a ready-made list of issues to research. It is not enough to know that you have a weakness; you need to understand why you have a weakness and then what you can do to correct it.

Rather than looking at weaknesses as facts and perceptions, it is better to look at them in light of the following:

- Does the brand have the proper resources to do the job?
- What perceptual barriers must be overcome to reach the objective?

The following are examples of weaknesses related to a lack of resources that could be devastating to a brand.

- The brand is losing money and has a mound of debt that has put it on the verge of bankruptcy. We have just seen this in the U.S. financial markets as huge companies and brands such as AIG collapsed. No matter what the brand vision, this is a high hurdle to overcome.
- The brand has produced goods that are so inferior that they are deemed a danger to society and are in the process of being banned from the market.
- The brand is shutting down factories and will not be able to make the brand.
- The brand has a management focus on milking the brand and no eye to grow it.
- The brand has been rejected by its key points of distribution.

You get the idea. Weaknesses are typically not this dire but you should be on the hunt for weaknesses that cannot be overcome. Typically these types of weaknesses are resource driven. When you review perceptual weaknesses, those can become real opportunities to turn a brand around. Many award-winning campaigns are built on overcoming an inherent weakness in the perception of the brand.

The following are examples of perceived brand weaknesses:

- Consumers feel that your brand is of no value.
- Consumers feel that your brand is not for them.
- Consumers feel that your brand is like everyone else's.
- Consumers don't recall the brand's advertising.
- Consumers don't like the brand's advertising.

These types of weaknesses are not insurmountable. Perceptions don't necessarily change overnight, but helping a brand become more relevant or using advertising the consumer likes is a far cry easier than working with a brand where management has no intention of supporting it. A savvy account planner will use the brand's perceptual weakness to see if there is an opportunity to reverse it. This is where great gains can be made through advertising.

External Assessment

Internal strengths and weaknesses focus on looking at the company and/or brand from the inside out. External strengths and weaknesses are opportunities and threats. Unlike internal strengths and weaknesses where you focus on the past and the present, external assessment focuses on the present and the future. Here you are looking for things that are happening or that you feel will happen that can influence the brand either positively or negatively.

The two big areas to assess for opportunities and/or threats are trends in the marketplace and competition. The role of the account planner is to assess consumer and cultural trends for the brand. Finding a connection between a cultural trend and the brand is one of the best ways to propel the brand forward. Conversely, trends can go against you. For example, if you are marketing a high-calorie indulgence and the trend is toward healthy snacks, then the brand may be facing an uphill battle.

However, capitalizing on trends can be a way to gain market share. In the economic downturn, Hyundai advertised that they help consumers who lost their jobs after buying a Hyundai car. By tapping into the consumer sentiment at the time—the fear of losing a job—Hyundai gained market share since consumers felt more confident about buying a Hyundai.

Competition is the second major aspect of an opportunity or a threat.

A weakness in the competition can create an opportunity for your brand. Conversely, a new competitor entering the marketplace can pose a severe threat. The future assessment of competition is one the account planner should actively take. You should be mindful of disruptive technologies or methods that can impact the market where there is none today. An example of this would be Netflix and Blockbuster. Renting a movie used to mean going to the store but Netflix changed that by creating a virtual storefront. This just underscores the need to take a present as well as a future view when analyzing opportunities and threats.

Opportunities

As you assess the opportunities available to the company, keep in mind that markets are dynamic and fresh opportunities continually evolve. You may want to set up criteria for short-term and longer-term opportunities. You may also want to look at trends that are competitive and trends that are consumer oriented.

For example, you may have identified out of your strength and weakness assessment that your competitor is retrenching and is pulling out of a market. This would signal a short-term opportunity to increase your share by filling that void. This is a great example of a short-term opportunity driven by competition.

But not all opportunities are as easy to see as this one. There are two layers of opportunity you want to identify for a company. The first layer encompasses the obvious opportunities, such as going after new geographic or target market segments or adding more product SKUs to the portfolio. The second layer goes deeper and entails understanding consumer trends and capitalizing on them.

For example, there is currently a consumer trend to be smart about eating carbohydrates. If you were a food manufacturer, this might lead you to develop a low-carbohydrate strategy in terms of new products and/or communications. This could lead to segmenting your audience differently than in the past. If your product fits in with this trend, you might use this opportunity as a tool to increase your price.

Trends as Opportunities

As an account planner, one of your central roles is to help clients understand what trends are emerging and how to capitalize on them. While that sounds like a noble mission, how do you actually spot trends?

There are a couple of paths you will want to take in seeking out trends.

The first path is to subscribe to trend research. The leading brand in the field of trends is Yankelovich, which has been studying the American consumer since 1971. The Yankelovich Monitor is a survey conducted on an annual basis serving many companies by looking into consumer attitudes, values, and lifestyles. Yankelovich conducts in-person, door-to-door interviews with 2,500 adults over the age of 16. This interview, coupled with a self-administered, leave-behind questionnaire, forms the basis for their ongoing tracking study that has been a mainstay in American culture for decades.

There are many other companies that focus on trends. One example is Iconoculture, a trend company offering a unique method of evaluating trends within the context of consumer values. Rather than fielding an ongoing study as Yankelovich does, Iconoculture relies on the input of 500 analysts who constantly feed a large database of consumer trends. These identified trends are then plotted against 120 consumer values and rolled up to a set of 36 macrotrends.

For example, one of the 36 macrotrends Iconoculture identifies is "Ready. Set. Go." This macrotrend is the combination of innovation plus convenience. A great example is Home Depot's plans to test convenience stores in its parking lots. For baby boomers, this macrotrend is an important ingredient to marketing to this group. The whole notion of convenience, access, and time is a cornerstone of baby boom values that rolls up to this trend. Understanding these types of trends can lead to new and better marketing as well as marketing communications.

Other companies focus on a specific market, such as kids, or a specific industry, such as food. All of these companies are great at offering the basic building blocks to understanding what trends might be emerging in society and how they might impact your client's brand.

Finally, you may want to do your own primary research with consumers. Motivational research techniques and ethnographic research are methods whereby researchers get at the deeper meanings that underlie a brand. This type of research, conducted over time, can help spot shifts in attitudes that can ultimately impact the client's brand or company.

Threats

If you are the brand manager of Tide laundry detergent and Clorox decides to launch a new laundry detergent brand that cleans twice as quickly as your brand, there is little doubt that this poses a threat to your brand.

Immediate threats like this are readily apparent. If you are on your toes, a move like this shouldn't come as a surprise. Threats can come from a variety of directions, so you should expand your thinking to beyond the standard competitive set when thinking about a competitive threat. It is often said your strengths are sometimes your greatest weaknesses. In looking at threats, it is a good idea to evaluate areas that may look positive but may come back to bite you in the rear.

For example, if you are a number three brand in your category, the distribution channel currently carrying your brand may turn out to be a larger threat than your competitor. With the rapid consolidation in the retail arena, private label brands from a Kroger in the grocery arena or a Home Depot in the home improvement market may be more of a threat to your existing shelf space than another manufacturer. So, the strength of being carried by a major retailer may turn into a threat if that retailer wants to market their version of the same item you manufacture.

In today's rapidly changing world, an online channel may change that dynamic balance of the marketplace and you could be on the outside looking in.

Another threat could come from how you make your product. If you are a coffee brand a shortage of coffee beans is a threat to your ability to put the brand on the shelf or sell it at a price that your customers can afford.

The latter threats are typically readily identified. Most companies have intelligence regarding their competition, distribution channels, and supply of raw materials. Even in a service business, such as airlines, shipping, retailing, or tax preparation, identifying competitive threats and potential cost issues is a matter of normal business intelligence gathering.

What separates the good brands from the great brands is identifying consumer trends that might be a threat to the business. For example, in early 2002 there was a trend toward eating fewer carbohydrates as a method to lose weight. This was started some 20 years earlier with the Atkins diet. Then, in 2002, the trend began to catch hold and become more mainstream. The South Beach diet, a friendlier Atkins diet, came into vogue and soon after stalwarts such as Weight Watchers and others were following suit. The potato, rice, and pasta industries were slow to respond and took a severe hit in short-term sales. Interestingly, this low-carb craze is a part of a larger trend identified by Iconoculture as "Wellville." Wellville seeks total well-being through the balance of self, community, and world. Although this may sound high and mighty, the notion of balance is the populist mantra among the baby boom generation. It played itself out in the low-carb craze where popular sentiment rallied against the no-carb crowd to say that a certain amount of carbs are good and there are good and bad carbs, much like there is good and bad cholesterol. The moral of this story is that if the potato, rice, and pasta group had followed this larger macrotrend and just fit into the overarching consumer trend, they would have not been as weakened as they were by fighting against the carb counters.

The SWOT analysis is a great tool for discussion and for setting the priorities among the opportunities the brand can take advantage of today and in the future. The action plans that come out of a SWOT analysis should include both a short-term goal to stem immediate threats or capitalize on immediate opportunities. The second action plan should be a longer-range plan that builds on the brand's strengths while working to shore up any glaring weaknesses. All of these future plans are worthless without a customer perspective, which is where you can add the most value to this exercise.

Organizational Storytelling

The SWOT analysis is predominantly a left-brained exercise. It is an assessment that is clinical by nature. While you can add some dimension to this exercise in the form of consumer knowledge, it is still largely analytical.

To balance out the SWOT analysis with something more right brained, you may want to embark upon drafting an organization narrative or story. Storytelling is becoming a more readily accepted method of helping management and marketing understand their company or brand.

A storyteller develops a story much in the same way a company develops a SWOT analysis. However, unlike a SWOT analysis, most stories are highly engaging. This is why innovative companies such as 3M are moving to storytelling as a method of business planning. The more engaging the plan, the better chance it will have of taking root in the organization.

The point of storytelling is to put a human face on what is a pretty clinical exercise. The greatest benefit of storytelling is that human beings naturally want to work through stories. Stories help us remember things better than to-do lists or the endless sea of PowerPoint presentations that come out of corporate America. "What is your story?" is something you may ask a new acquaintance. The same is true in business.

The first step in telling a company's story is to define the company as the protagonist. To paint a picture of the company you must understand its strengths (the S in SWOT) and values. Then, the storyteller determines what the protagonist wants or desires. Desire is the lifeblood of any story. Is the brand's desire to be the best or known as the best, to move into new markets, or to squash a competitor? The company's desires are essentially the opportunities outlined in the SWOT.

The plot is built on the company's quest to seek opportunity; it must overcome weaknesses and slay outside threats to reach the goal. Once the basis for the story is set, the storyteller's next job is to decide how the protagonist should act to achieve these desires in the face of antagonistic forces. It is in the answer to that question that storytellers reveal the truth about their characters. Most characters are revealed in the choices they make in their lives.

Let's reverse the process a bit and tell the story of Hansel and Gretel as a SWOT analysis. (We assume you know the story of Hansel and Gretel and the evil witch. If not, check out some children's books.) Hansel and Gretel had the character strengths of being clever, which led them to leave a breadcrumb trail so they wouldn't get lost. They had to overcome the weaknesses of being alone and overcoming their fears. The evil witch was a major threat as were birds eating the breadcrumb trail and the dark forest. But Hansel and Gretel prevailed and got not only the food but some gold coins to boot.

Now let's look at how to tell a story of a company. Waste Management, a trash and waste removal company, had a poor reputation with accounting scandals and past associations with gangsters in the trash hauling business. However, under new leadership, Waste Management was reinventing itself as an environmental services company known for innovation. Waste Management was a leader in recycling and in using landfills to develop methane gas as a fuel alternative. But the company was reluctant to tell their story for fear of bringing up the past transgressions. They were also not sure that customers would really care about their story. But, through a series of events their story was told with the positive publicity helping to change public opinions. Here is one small segment of it:

Imagine this story. "One day the leader of the world's greatest environmental company decided everyone should know what great things the company was doing. Although many told him to be quiet, he just could not for he was proud of his associates' accomplishments. So he rang bells and handed out advertisements that told of the wondrous things the company was doing to help its customers and the earth. And the people were amazed and rejoiced. They had no idea that great things had been going on for so long. Not only did they think better of the company, they also paid handsomely for its services."

Your story can be a summary or it can be a very long story that details specific events and chronicles specific strengths, weaknesses, threats, and opportunities. It is largely up to you. The point of the storytelling exercise is to dramatize the outcome the company is trying to achieve and to put a more human face on what can be a rather dry exercise.

Review Questions

1. Explain the process for a situational analysis.
2. Define the acronym SWOT.

3. Does SWOT cover all the elements that are needed for a situational analysis?
4. How does the wheel of competitive strategy (Figure 4.2) assist the marketing manager with an IMC campaign?

Discussion Questions

1. Why is a situational analysis so important?
2. What problems might occur if situational analysis is not performed?
3. How does SWOT help a marketing campaign?

Additional Resources

Anderson, E. *Being Strategic: Plan for Success—Out-Think Your Competitors—Stay Ahead of Change.* New York: St. Martin's Press, 2009.
Steel, J. *Perfect Pitch: The Art of Selling Ideas and Winning New Business.* Hoboken, NJ: Wiley, 2006.

Chapter 5

Benchmarking Consumer Perceptions

To understand where the brand is today in the consumer's mind, you need to conduct some research. At this stage of the process, you want to benchmark consumer perceptions so that when you launch your campaign, you will have measures to compare precampaign to postcampaign. Benchmarking consumer perceptions is a key aspect of developing your brand roadmap.

Before you develop any advertising campaign, you want to know the fundamentals of the consumer's interaction with the brand. Your research should be designed to answer questions such as:

- How many people know about the brand?
- How many people buy the brand?
- What do they think about the brand?
- What are the barriers to growing the brand?

Answering these questions will help form the foundation for the SWOT analysis. Coupled with the secondary information that we described in the Chapter 4, you should be well on your way to understanding the situation.

In developing an award-winning campaign, you must look at the brand from the consumer perspective. And that is what benchmarking consumer perceptions will help you do. However, understanding the consumer is a means to an end. The ultimate goal is to help grow the brand. It is important to translate consumer behavior and perceptions into something actionable for the client. One way to look at the information is to develop a brand purchase funnel.

Purchase Funnel

A brand purchase funnel diagrams the steps that a consumer takes in the brand purchase process. Figure 5.1 shows a traditional brand purchase funnel. The purchase funnel can also begin to construct what role advertising will play in solving the brand's marketing problems.

Figure 5.1   **Awareness-to-Loyalty Funnel Diagram**

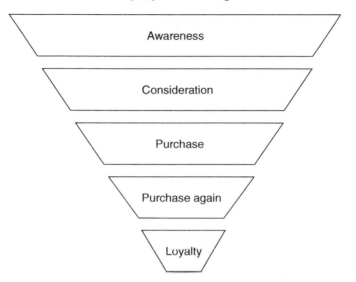

In the traditional purchase funnel shown in Figure 5.1, *awareness* is at the top of the funnel. This means that the first step to getting someone to purchase the brand is for them to be aware of it. That makes sense. Who would buy a product without knowing about it? Once they are aware of the brand, the second stage is *consideration;* will someone consider the brand when they have a need for it? That leads to the third stage, *purchase.* This is pretty simple. After weighing the choices or considerations, do consumers buy your brand or not? The fourth stage is *purchase again.* Once a consumer buys your brand, will they buy it again? The final stage of the purchase funnel is *loyalty.* This is measured a number of ways. One is exclusivity. Is this the only brand that the consumer will buy in this category? Will no other brand do? Another way is by fame. Is this a brand that the consumer is so in love with that they will rave about it to other people?

As you can see, the purchase funnel assumes a logical flow from being aware of the brand to considering the brand to purchasing the brand to purchasing it again and finally to buying only that brand. Just imagine trying to fill a bucket with water by using a funnel. The more water you place at the wider end of the funnel, the more you get out of the bottom. The same concept is held forth here with consumers. The more consumers who are aware of your brand, the more will consider it and then buy it and buy it again. While there are different purchase funnels for different brands and situations, the components of the purchase funnel are always fundamentally the same. This is why the purchase funnel is popular with companies and

Figure 5.2   **Coca-Cola Purchase Funnel**

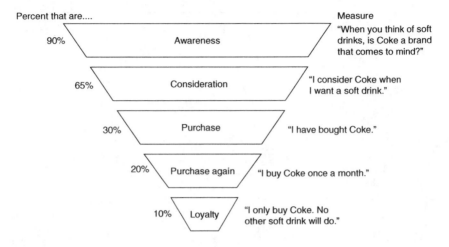

brands. It is easy to communicate to senior management. And it can be a nice diagnostic tool for determining whether there are bottlenecks or barriers that might impact the flow of the funnel.

Assuming that you are filling the consumer bucket, then the first thing you need to understand is the awareness level of the brand. Figure 5.2 is a consumer perspective of the purchase funnel using Coke as an example. There are two things to notice about Figure 5.2. First is that each aspect of the purchase funnel is put in consumer language rather than in brand language. Second, you can begin to understand the dimensions of the purchase funnel by the metrics for each stage and the relationship between the data.

As you walk through the hypothetical purchase funnel dynamics for Coke, you see that virtually everyone has heard of Coke. Ninety percent of consumers think of Coke when asked about soft drinks. However, in this case, only 65 percent consider Coke when they want a soft drink. So there is a drop-off in consideration. Then, thirty percent actually purchase Coke; basically, one out two people who consider Coke will buy it. Twenty percent purchase Coke more than once and 10 percent buy Coke exclusively. Now you know that two-thirds of consumers who buy a Coke will buy another and one-third of Coke drinkers drink Coke exclusively.

This raises a number of research and advertising issues. You know that virtually everyone has heard of Coke, so generating awareness of the brand isn't much of an issue. However, 35 percent of consumers do not consider Coke when they want a soft drink. That raises questions of why not, and an advertising issue of how to get this group to consider Coke. Only one out of every two people who consider buying a Coke actually buys one. Again,

Figure 5.3   **Purchase Funnel Dynamics: Internet Impact**

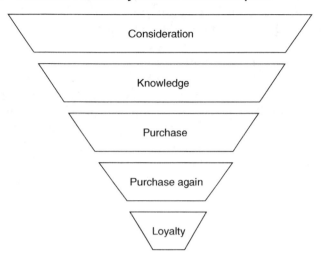

why doesn't the other half buy Coke? From an advertising standpoint, can we convince them to buy Coke once it is in the consideration set? Armed with the data that two-thirds of Coke drinkers will drink more than one Coke and one-third only drink Coke, you could consider research that would lead to a frequency program to gain more usage from current Coke drinkers.

The purchase funnel is a great tool for framing the marketing and advertising issues that may face a brand. It is a simple tool that can demonstrate to management what needs to be done and how marketing and advertising works to gain more new users and more frequent users of the brand.

Purchase Funnel Dynamics

For many retail brands, the purchase funnel serves as a good model for the consumer dynamics of buying behavior. However, for brands that are purchased infrequently or are costly, there may be a different dynamic. This type of purchase coupled with the rise of the Internet as a retail channel and information resource has led to a new understanding of the purchase funnel.

In many cases, consumers now put consideration at the top of the purchase funnel with awareness second. Figure 5.3 demonstrates this change in the purchase funnel dynamics. The fundamental change in consumer dynamics moves from thinking of brands they might consider to going online to find as many brands as possible to consider. The Internet allows consumers to vastly increase their consideration set compared to just recalling brands. Once consumers have found all the possible options to solve their problem, then they fine tune the consideration set by how much they know about the brand. This second step begins with awareness of the brand ("Have I heard of it?") but rapidly advances to, "What do I know about"?

The health care, automotive, and insurance industries are all good examples of this change in consumer behavior. The consumer will look online first to find out all the possible options to fit a need. Then he or she will whittle it down to a smaller set based on awareness and knowledge of the brand, and then make a purchase decision. The implication of this from a marketing and advertising perspective is enormous. Instead of beginning with just awareness, a brand should begin with ensuring that they are in the broader consideration set. This may lead to a strategy of awareness and also a deeper online presence. Or it may lead to a strategy of driving consumers to a Web site to gain a deeper knowledge of the brand.

A similar chain of diagnostics can be developed but it may be more multidimensional than the one-way flow of the traditional purchase funnel.

Benchmarking Research

To benchmark how the consumer feels about your brand you will need to conduct primary research. The primary research study that is typically conducted in either a professional or a student plan is an Awareness, Attitude, and Usage (AAU) study. This research helps you understand where you are today and will serve as a benchmark for measuring your progress toward your goal. An AAU study can also provide information to help you segment your target market.

Let's review each aspect of an AAU study and what the implications are for developing a campaign.

Brand Awareness

First and foremost for any brand is to be known. Most people don't buy something that they know nothing about. A key measure of a brand is the public's awareness of it. Brand awareness has various levels: unaided awareness and its subset, top-of-mind awareness, and aided awareness and its subset, familiarity.

Unaided brand awareness is when a consumer can remember and play back your brand without being prompted. A question to determine unaided brand awareness in the soft drink category could be, "When you think of soft drinks, which brand first comes to mind?" Consumers might answer, "Coke." A researcher may follow up with, "Are there any other brands that come to mind?" Consumers may answer, "Pepsi." In this case, both Coke and Pepsi would have unaided brand awareness.

Top-of-mind awareness is that coveted position where a consumer thinks of your brand first when discussing a category. In our prior example, we said that Coke and Pepsi were the two brands that came to mind. The consumer's first response was Coke. That is an example of top-of-mind awareness. Many researchers refer to this as "first mention," or the brand that first comes to mind. Top-of-mind awareness is a subset of unaided awareness.

The reason unaided awareness and particularly top-of-mind awareness is so coveted is that research has shown a high correlation between these factors and a brand's market share. Brands that lead the category in terms of awareness many times are also the market share leaders in that category.

The next level is aided awareness. While Dr. Pepper may not immediately come to mind, if you asked consumers if they have heard of Dr. Pepper many would probably say yes. In aided awareness the consumer is prompted to acknowledge whether they have heard of a specific brand or company.

A subset of aided awareness is brand familiarity. This is as simple as it sounds. Do consumers just know the name of the brand or are they very familiar with it? There is a big difference between just jogging someone's memory with the name of the brand and getting feedback about what the brand's personality.

The level of awareness of the brand helps to determine what problem you have to solve. If no one knows about the brand, then you need to generate awareness. If consumers know the name and nothing else, then you have a knowledge problem and you need to educate consumers about what the brand stands for or how it is unique. Each facet of the AAU can help guide you on how to frame the problem that advertising must solve.

Advertising Awareness

Just like brand awareness, there are similar measures for advertising awareness. For example, you may ask consumers to tell you what soft drink advertising they have recently seen or heard. Advertising awareness may not be the same as brand awareness. For example, if Sprite has just introduced a new advertising campaign, consumers may indicate that they have seen Sprite advertising even though Coke may be their top-of-mind brand awareness choice.

Just like brand awareness, you want to ask consumers if they have seen advertising for your brand. This is an example of aided awareness. Familiarity with the brand's advertising is measured by how much a consumer can recall or remember about the advertising. Can they play back the main message of the advertising? Do they recall any specifics about it? Do they link the specific advertising with the brand or do they confuse it with another? For example, if a consumer plays back a Pepsi commercial and ties it to Coke, then you know that your commercial is not linked properly with the brand.

All of these measures are central to diagnosing what problem you have to solve with your communications effort.

Attitude

Consumers may not consider your brand or buy it because they are not aware of it. However, for the great majority of situations, the reason a consumer may not buy or even consider your brand is based on some perception or belief held about the brand. That is where attitudinal questions come into play. The following are the key attitudinal issues that should be addressed in the AAU:

- What is important to the consumer about this category? What factors drive the purchase decision?
- How does the brand deliver on those important factors?
- How does the brand compare to others in the category on these factors?
- What does the consumer think about the brand?

The goal of this aspect of the AAU is to understand what barriers you need to overcome with advertising to help move the brand toward its goal.

Every category has certain characteristics that are crucial when making a buying decision. In the soft drink category, taste is a big component. In choosing a grocery store, fresh produce may be important. When buying gasoline, price and convenience may be important. Whatever category you are measuring, there are certain fundamental factors, such as product quality, price, and convenience.

Once you understand the factors, then you can see how your brand delivers on them and how you may compare to other brands in the category. This will give you a measure of worth and relative worth on each attribute. For example, if you were analyzing the difference between Kroger and Walmart in the grocery sector, you might consider price, convenience, fresh produce, service, quality of the bakery, and cleanliness of store as attributes. If you found that Kroger ranked low on price but high on everything else, you might consider a campaign that stresses quality, service, and freshness over price. Or you may have a way to combat price using a loyalty card versus Walmart's everyday low-price strategy. The point is that these attributes can become key items for how you build a campaign.

The other aspect of perceptions is to find out what consumers think about your brand on an emotional level. For example, do they think that your store is for old people or that it is hip and modern? Do consumers associate your brand with being sophisticated or homey? Is it feminine or masculine? The brand's awareness of these perceptions is important and leads to a firm understanding of what is in the mind of the consumer.

Usage Measures

You want to understand who is using your brand and how often they are using it. The usage measures of the AAU survey cover those aspects. The usage measures are designed to help you fill in the consideration, purchase, repeat purchase, and loyalty portions of the purchase funnel.

Going back to our Coke example, you would want to find out if someone considers Coke when buying a soft drink. That gets at the considered set. From there, you would want to know what brands of soft drinks they buy. This may include Coke and other brands as well. If they consume Coke, you would likely want to know if they are drinking it two or three times a day or just once a week. So, a scaling question that gets to frequency of usage is an important element of usage measures.

To get at a measure of loyalty, you could ask Coke drinkers if they use that brand exclusively or if they drink other soft drinks. Another way to gauge loyalty is to directly ask the consumer if it is their favorite brand. The question you want to answer is how committed the consumer is to your brand. Are they raving fans or do they just like it?

Based on what you learn from usage questions, you can begin to address advertising issues, as we have detailed in going over the purchase funnel measures.

Comparing Different Audiences

Now that you have completed the AAU, it is time to analyze the results. If you have a professional research company conducting the survey, you would ask for them to cross-tabulate the data. If you are a student doing a survey for the NSAC competition, you are likely to be using software such as Survey Monkey, which can filter data. Whether you are asking for cross-tabulations or filtering data on your own, you want to look for stories within the data. Typically those stories come from looking at the differences between audiences.

Most researchers want to assess the following different sets of audiences to see if a pattern emerges.

- Consumers who are aware of your brand and those who are not aware.
- Consumers who are very familiar with your brand and those who are not.
- Consumers who consider your brand and those that don't consider it at all.
- Consumers who use or buy your brand and those who do not.
- Consumers who are frequent users of your brand and those who are just casual users.

- Consumers who are aware of your advertising and those who are not.
- Consumers who like your advertising and those who do not.

By using these questions, you can discover the demographic and attitudinal differences of each audience. For example, if you found that men were less aware of Coke and its advertising than women, that might suggest a strategy. Or discovering that one group loves the brand and another hates it might suggest another approach. The one research danger in cross tabbing information is to make sure that you have a sample large enough so that the information is credible. Most researchers consider a sample size of 100 per cell as a reliable number for forming a conclusion. A cell size of 100 likely means that the overall sample of the study could be well over 1,000 respondents. As you conduct this study, you should consult with either a professional researcher or a research text to guide you on proper sampling methodology. We have listed one at the end of this chapter for your reference.

Benchmarking the consumer's perception of the brand and its advertising is the cornerstone to developing a strong situation analysis and can lead to ideas for segmenting your market. It is the initial step on the way to the final brand destination.

Review Questions

1. What is the purchase funnel? Why is it important?
2. How has the Internet changed the purchase funnel dynamics?
3. What is the AAU survey? Why is it important?
4. What are the different levels of awareness?
5. What are different aspects of brand usage?
6. What makes up attitudinal aspects of the AAU?

Discussion Questions

1. What are other ways to capture consumer behavior dynamics other than the purchase funnel?
2. Are there brands for which the purchase funnel dynamic doesn't work?
3. Are there measures outside the AAU that should be considered to measure a brand's situation?
4. Does the AAU capture the emotional connection of a brand?

Additional Resource

Jugenheimer, D., S. Bradley, L. Kelley, L., and J. Hudson. *Advertising and Public Relations Research.* Armonk, NY: M.E. Sharpe, 2010.

Chapter 6

Understanding the Consumer Mind-Set

Asking consumers questions on a survey will tell you how they may think about a brand. But a survey on its own won't really tell you why they think that way. The majority of buying decisions are made based on emotional rather than rational reasons. Surveys are great at capturing rational measures of a brand such as awareness, usage, or intent to use, and even some fundamental attitudes towards a brand, but it can't capture deep-seated emotions. That is why you need qualitative research to work in tandem with a quantitative study.

The AAU, which was discussed in the previous chapter, may lead you to identify a marketing or advertising problem. For example, if 60 percent of consumers consider Coke but only 30 percent actually purchase it, you know that there is a conversion problem but you don't know why. Qualitative research is designed to get at those whys. Properly conducted qualitative research can help you understand the consumer's mind-set, which will lead to developing insights and an effective advertising campaign.

Qualitative research differs from quantitative research in some fundamental ways:

- Quantitative research is designed to gain statistically significant data that requires a large sample size, while qualitative research is designed to gauge emotions using a relatively small sample that is not statistically projectable.
- Qualitative research is typically conducted so that you can see and hear a consumer, while quantitative research is conducted anonymously.
- Qualitative research is designed for open-ended questions that require judgment to interpret, while quantitative research is designed for closed response and scales that require analysis.

Qualitative research is a key element in account planning and developing advertising campaigns. In fact, account planners often conduct their own qualitative research to gain deeper insights into the consumer's mind-set.

There are a number of methods and techniques used to gain this understanding. This discussion considers some of the more popular techniques used in award-winning campaigns.

Types of Qualitative Studies

When someone mentions qualitative research, the first thing that comes to mind is conducting a focus group. Focus groups are a popular method for getting reactions from consumers. But there are other popular qualitative research methods beyond a traditional focus group. This chapter focuses on the following types of studies:

- Focus groups and iterations of them
- Online communities
- Projective exercises
- Zaltman Metaphor Elicitation Technique (ZMET)
- Ethnographic research

Conducting a focus group or groups is a typical method used by advertisers from idea generation to creative testing. Focus groups traditionally are held in a facility and watched in person by the client and agency through a two-way mirror. However, the Internet is changing this process. Online communities, groups connected only through the Internet or other electronic means, can actually conduct a focus group online rather than in person, using the Internet connection to substitute for face-to-face contact. To make the use of a focus group or an online community more valuable, marketers have come up with a wide variety of projective exercises that help get after the deeper emotional nature of what the consumer is thinking. Olson Zaltman Associates developed ZMET to access to deep emotions through what they call deep metaphor research.

All of these techniques are designed to get a reaction from consumers and to more deeply understand their motivations and perceptions of your brand.

Focus Groups

Focus groups are the traditional method for conducting in-person surveys. A focus group usually consists of eight to twelve respondents who are recruited by an advertising agency. These groups are conducted at facilities equipped with conference rooms with two-way mirrors, where clients and agency personnel eat M&M's and watch the dialogue unfold. These discussions are led by a skilled moderator and last approximately 90 minutes.

To get a lot out of focus groups, you need a skilled moderator who can get the group of strangers to interact. This is no easy trick. To generate deeper insights, it is always a good idea to have focus group members with contrasting dynamics. For example, the University of Houston National Student Advertising Competition (NSAC) competition class conducted a focus group with men and another with women to see if there were differences in gender attitudes toward binge drinking. Figure 6.1 shows the keywords that each group used to describe their experiences with binge drinking. Comparing the lists, you can see that there was a big difference between the two, which led to a specific way to target advertising.

Finding out the difference between brand users, competitive users, and category non-users is typically very enlightening. Focus groups can help to isolate differences among target groups. Categories can include usage, gender, age, and/or geography.

Focus groups can be problematic, however. Researchers question the true insights that are possible within a focus-group setting for the following reasons:

- The discussion takes place in an unnatural setting. Participants know they are being watched, which can lead to opinions that may not reflect their true feelings. They may either feel too timid to express themselves or they may want to show off for the client.
- The focus group participants are interacting with people they don't know so it is difficult to get at deep feelings.
- The participants are participating for the money, which creates a much different mind-set than just talking about a brand with no incentive.
- Because there are eight to twelve respondents, the moderator is forced to get surface answers to ensure that everyone participates. At best, each participant speaks for about seven minutes in a ninety-minute session.

These issues have led researchers to create variations on traditional focus groups. To reduce the size yet maintain some degree of interaction, some focus groups have gone to smaller formats. Triads, or three-person focus groups, are one popular alternative. One-on-one interviews are also a popular method. The smaller the group, the deeper the moderator can probe into issues.

Online Communities

Research companies have moved aggressively into using online tools for research. This move has led to a number of innovations regarding qualita-

Figure 6.1   Research Diagram

Research

Our Research Objectives Are:

- Understand how students feel about drinking.
- Understand situations in which students frequently binge drink.
- Gain insight into words students associate with binge drinking.
- Understand the differences between the way men and women drink.
- Gain insight into some of the more common consequences students suffer when they binge drink.

Primary Research

For our research we did an Internet study, word association, mind mapping, storytelling and cartooning. Following are our results:

Internet Survey (1000 respondents)

The term binge was equated with wasted.

There are major differences between men and women when it comes to the amount of alcohol consumed.

Storytelling (50 respondents)

Women have memories and experiences that they often regret. Men do not.

Mind Mapping (200 respondents)

Women associate going out and having fun with drinking alcohol, whereas men are more inclined to hang out at home.

Cartooning (200 respondents)

Overall, men exhibited a more casual outlook on drinking. Women made it clear that drinking is social and empowering to them, but they also had many negative responses.

Word Association (200 respondents)

Women and men have their own individual ideas about drinking.

Women associate more negative terms with overconsumption than men.

Too Much to Drink

Female	Male
Love	Good times
Tylenol	Weekends
Binge drinking	Friendly
Hangover	Sex
Cigarettes	Partying
Pictures	Fun
Toilet	Patron
Vomit	Birthday
Falling	Jello Shots
Another drink	Singing
Floor	Happy
Silly	Beer
	Once in a while
	Dancing

tive research. The two key areas are stretching time and the broadening the audience.

Traditional focus groups are limited in that you only get a snapshot of a consumer's viewpoint in a small amount of time. At best, qualitative researchers may spend an hour or two with a consumer. While a lot can be accomplished in this time, deeper understanding could be gained if you could spend a week, a month, or more with consumers.

An online community may consist of 10 to 100 members who agree to participate in an ongoing research study. They may be recruited to participate for a day, a week, or more, depending on the brand's needs. This consumer group functions more as an advisory panel than a focus group. This gives the brand an opportunity to really learn how the members think and to dive much deeper into issues. The virtual nature of the community allows the members more control over their time so they respond to questions or discussion whenever it is convenient for them.

This type of panel can be conducted using online chat rooms or to give respondents online assignments that they can return to the researcher in a few days. For example, you may ask members of your panel to go to the grocery store and buy your brand and then prepare a meal with it. Then you can find out about their experience with the brand from the purchase of the brand to consumption. This can offer rich qualitative feedback.

Another benefit of an online panel or community is the ability to use a much larger sample size than with a traditional focus group. A brand community can be constructed so that you have wide-ranging geographical representation and can include as many as 100 members. Numbers should be limited to no more than 100, however, or the community can lose its ability to interact.

Online communities are not inexpensive but there is flexibility in how they can be used. When fielding a number of studies, the online community becomes cost-effective compared with conducting a variety of independent research projects.

The downside to virtual focus groups is the inability to read a person's facial responses. While there is the opportunity to do live chat with a camera, it is not the same as actually being in the same room with the respondent. Online communities do rely greatly on a consumer's ability to communicate through writing. By its very nature writing can provide a more rational response to a question because the respondent has more time to consider and compile the response.

As technology advances, new and innovative methods for engaging consumers in dialogue come about. Online communities should be taken into consideration when you embark upon doing qualitative research.

Projective Techniques

The goal of qualitative research is to get at the emotional nature of the human response to your brand or your advertising. Yet most consumers either cannot articulate their emotions or may not be fully aware of what they are. To get at these deeper levels of emotion, advertising has taken a page from psychology. Psychologists use projective techniques to help them with clinical diagnosis. One familiar projective technique is the Rorschach test, in which people look at inkblots and project what they see.

Psychologist and marketing expert Ernest Dichter is regarded by many as the "father of motivational research." He pioneered the application of projective techniques in the advertising and marketing world in the 1950s. In fact, Vance Packard's 1956 book *The Hidden Persuaders* contains references to Ditcher's work and its influence in advertising.

The underlying premise of projective techniques is that it is difficult to obtain accurate information about what a person thinks and feels just by asking them. By allowing a person to project their thoughts and feelings onto something else—another person, object, or situation—they can better explain their feelings.

There are a number of projective techniques that can provide insight. Some of the preferred methods include the following:

- Mind mapping
- Word association
- Picture storytelling
- Cartooning
- Sentence completion

Mind mapping allows a consumer to visualize their total view of the brand in a free-form exercise. Figure 6.2 shows an example of a mind map created by the University of Texas NSAC competition team for a competition with Coke as the client. The mind map begins as a simple map with the brand at the center with key areas you want the consumer to address. In the case of Coke, the student group wanted to find out the associations consumers had with the brand's image, its advertising, memories of using the brand, and its sensory feelings. The map is extended to incorporate the consumer's responses and a facilitator coaches the respondent to continue each thought outward to completion. For example, when respondents associated Coke with friends, the facilitator asked about the situations in which the respondent drank a Coke while with friends. In this case, answers ranged from chugging contests to just breaking the ice with someone. You can use this technique to get at a deeper level of knowledge about the brand. It is also effective to combine individual mind maps into a composite like the one shown in Figure 6.2.

Word association is a simple projective technique that can be used to get at deeper emotional levels. You can either give consumers words and suggest responses that the respondent chooses from or use "free association" in which no suggested responses are provided. This exercise is useful in comparing one brand to another to see if they occupy the same space in consumer's minds or if there are big differences in perception.

Projective techniques are intended to insert the respondents into the research story. Picture storytelling is a visual projective technique that can illustrate an individual's feelings about a brand and can be done individually or in a group. For this exercise, you ask consumers to bring in pictures that symbolize their attitudes and feelings toward the brand and its competition. Then the consumer tells a story about why they selected these images to represent their brand experience. For example, when consumers were asked to compare International House of Pancakes (IHOP) to Denny's, the pictures were startlingly different. IHOP fostered delicious food pictures while Denny's generated pictures of people having a good time. It was obvious that IHOP was more about indulgence and Denny's was more about camaraderie.

In Jon Steel's book *Perfect Pitch,* the author describes how he used cartooning to reveal why consumers wouldn't buy a Porsche automobile. He asked non-Porsche owners to fill in a cartoon that asked them to imagine themselves sitting in their car at a stoplight next to a Porsche 911. Figure 6.3 captures that reaction. From this insight, Steel went on to define the problem as follows: "Consumers do not want to buy one of your cars because they are scared by what their friends and perfect strangers alike will think of them."

Keep in mind what projective techniques are intended to do. Developing situations for the consumer allows them to project their feelings and attitudes in a noninvasive way.

A more straightforward projective technique is sentence completion. In this exercise you ask a consumer to fill in the blank. Just like cartooning, it is a good exercise to help consumers describe what others might think of them if they used a certain brand. For example, if you were doing a sentence completion exercise for Porsche, you might have consumers fill in the blanks on the following sentences:

- If I purchased a Porsche, my friends would say _____.
- People who drive Porsches are _____.
- Porsches are for people who are _____.

62

Figure 6.2 Mind Map

mind map

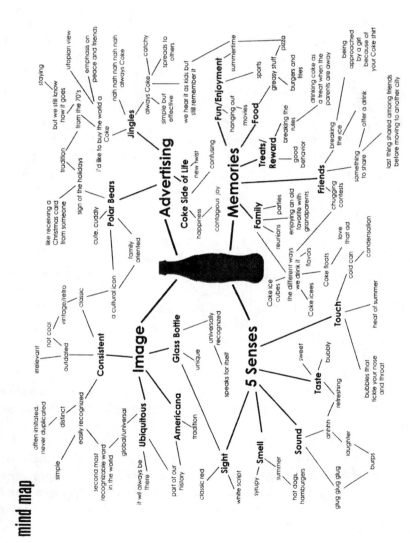

Figure 6.3 **Cartoon showing the reaction of an ordinary American driver to the driver of a Porsche**

This technique is directly lifted from psychology. It offers consumers a way to project their feelings about a brand in an indirect manner.

All of these projective techniques are designed to help consumers display deeper levels of thinking. The use of projective techniques is especially important in the development of creative ideas and expression.

ZMET

Few people know more about using metaphors to understand consumers than Gerald Zaltman, Professor Emeritus at Harvard Business School, author of more than twenty books, and founder of the marketing research firm Olson Zaltman Associates. ZMET, patented by Olson Zaltman Associates, delves into the subconscious thinking that drives consumer behavior.

Deep metaphors are subconscious thoughts that affect how people process and react to information or brands; they manifest themselves in everyday language and conversation. For example, a consumer may refer to a cell phone as a lifeline or a man may describe motor oil as his truck's lifeblood. These are examples of one of seven giant metaphors that Zaltman characterizes in his book *Marketing Metaphoria.* In this case, the cell phone as a lifeline and motor oil as lifeblood fall under an overarching metaphor of resources that consumers utilize in their everyday lives. The ZMET technique elicits metaphors using a series of steps and nondirective probing. Then the metaphors are grouped together so the researcher can surmise what a person is using to frame or understand a topic. This technique is a powerful tool for getting at the "whys" behind the "what" of consumer behavior.

Ethnographic Research

Much of the aforementioned research is conducted by recruiting consumers to a facility and talking to them in a fairly clinical environment, or utilizing online research. Projective techniques help consumers give away more of themselves than they probably would in a focus group. The current trend is to turn the tables and bring the research to the consumers.

Ethnography is the study of human culture. It involves direct first-hand observation of daily behavior. Researchers can watch consumers from afar, such as by nonintrusive observations or even small television systems, or actually live in their homes for a few days. The idea is to get into the consumer's environment and watch their daily routines. Many marketers use ethnographic research to immerse themselves into the lives of their consumers.

The goal of ethnography is to observe how a consumer interacts with a brand in a natural setting. A study by the advertising agency for Wrangler Jeans found that men who bought twelve or more pairs of jeans in a year had a pecking order for their jeans. There were work jeans, date jeans, casual jeans, sports jeans, and even formal jeans. From this information, the agency began to craft a strategy that appealed to all of these situations.

Summary

Gaining insights from qualitative research forms the foundation for developing award-winning campaigns. While you can isolate a problem using quantitative surveys, it usually takes deeper probing to find out the reason why behind the "what" of consumer behavior. Whether it is through a focus group, one on one, an online panel, or in-depth interviews, it is important to get at the emotional level of the consumer. That is where using projective techniques comes into play. In the Chapter 7, we discuss what insights are and how they lead to advertising campaigns.

Review Questions

1. What is the difference between quantitative and qualitative research?
2. What are the different forms of qualitative research?

3. What are projective techniques? How are they used in research?
4. What is the difference between ethnographic and other qualitative research methods?

Discussion Questions

1. Can you develop an effective advertising campaign without using qualitative research?
2. How do you blend quantitative and qualitative research to learn about the consumer?
3. What do you think are the best ways to use projective techniques?

Additional Resources

DeBono, E. *Lateral Thinking: Creativity Step by Step.* New York: Harper & Row, 1973.
Dru. J. *Beyond Disruption: Changing the Rules in the Marketplace.* New York: Wiley, 2002.
Dru, J. *Disruption: Overturning Conventions and Shaking Up the Marketplace.* New York: Wiley, 1996.
Steel, J. *Perfect Pitch: The Art of Selling Ideas and Winning New Business.* Hoboken, NJ: Wiley, 2007.

Chapter 7
Developing Insights

What Is an Insight?

Account planning is driven by finding insights into problems and their solutions. Great marketing and communication campaigns are founded on great insights. People use the word "insight" all the time. Yet what is an insight? We might define an insight as the ability to see and understand clearly the inner nature of things. Or it is the clear understanding of a specific thing or the awareness of one's own mental attitudes and behaviors.

In essence, it is essential that we find and understand "why" we behave the way we do. For account planners and anyone seeking insights to develop an award-winning campaign it also involves looking at things differently. It requires seeing things intuitively, a power the Greeks called *noesis*. This power is the ability of acute observation, deduction, penetration, and discernment. It is looking at relationships in a new and unique way.

A true insight into consumer behavior will connect with the consumer at an emotional level. It will provoke a clear response such as "that is exactly how I feel," or "this brand really understands me," or "I've never thought about it that way." When you connect with a consumer in this way it can affect a change in consumer behavior that benefits your brand.

Where to Look for Insights

So how does one gain insight? Award-winning campaigns are built on insights from any number of sources, but they all revolve around the consumer, the brand, and the advertising. Here are seven insight areas that you should explore when developing a campaign.

- The product's reason for being
- The product's history
- How consumers use the product

- How brand consumers see themselves
- Untapped belief about the product
- Barrier to using the product
- Category and brand advertising

Each of these areas may contain insights that have not yet seen the light of day. All are fruitful areas to explore for insight.

The Product's Reason for Being

The first place to start is with the brand itself. It was designed to help consumers solve a problem. What is that problem and how do consumers feel about it? In his book *Creative Insight: The Researcher's Art,* Jeffrey Durgee terms this insight area "the product and its object." For example, mouthwash was designed to kill germs in your mouth. However, that isn't all that it does. The mouth can be a gross storage area for disgusting germs but it can be a sensuous part of the body. Some mouthwash brands take a clinical approach to their brand and advertising while others take a more personal interaction approach. The best place to start is with the general needs of the consumer with regard to the product category. Usually the category leader will be aligned with the overall benefit of the category. In this case, Listerine started with a campaign that mocked its taste with their campaign, the worse it tastes, the better it works to keep your breath smelling fresh. It migrated from there to take the clinical turf of killing germs and then to killing germs to keep gums healthier and onward to killing germs to keep you away from a poor dentist visit. All of these were based on insights about the product itself and how consumers interacted with it.

History of the Product

Brands that have been around awhile have a history and consumers have a history with the brand. Past experience and personal history of the brand is highly relevant and a great place to look for insights. One of the most interesting places to look for insights in this category is the "first time."

Whether it is a first kiss or your first car, first-time experiences are typically packed with emotions. This can be fertile ground for finding a nugget of insight into an advertising campaign.

For example, the advertising campaign for St. Pauli Girl beer directly plays into the idea of associating with first experiences with its themeline "You never forget your first Girl." St. Pauli Girl's advertising lets readers use their own imagination so all the visuals in the campaign encourage the audience members to tell their own stories.

Another example of tapping into the history of a brand was in an IPA award-winning KFC ad by London-based advertising agency BBH. Many users of KFC and other fast food restaurants were becoming more health conscious and reducing how often they bought fast food.

KFC suffered a double whammy, since the majority of their business comes from moms feeding their families. These moms prefer to provide healthy choices for dinner. So instead of promoting healthier products in the KFC lineup, BBH went back to KFC's roots: the unique taste and indulgence of KFC's Original Recipe fried chicken. Qualitative research showed that moms loved the taste and knew that they couldn't make it themselves.

BBH's campaign created food desire and reminded people of what they loved about KFC. The reward for moms was that everyone loves KFC, so dinnertime could be a success. By tapping into the origins of KFC, BBH was able to increase brand penetration in a weak fast food marketplace.

How Users See Themselves

Another area that abounds in insights is how brand users see themselves. Often a brand is a reflection the self. A classic example of this is Harley-Davidson riders, who see themselves as independent sorts even if they are accountants during the week. Harley-Davidson has done a tremendous job of capturing that mystique. People who want to be associated with a more rebellious side of their lives can tap into it by buying and riding a Harley.

Consumers view themselves in relationship to the brands they use. Some people would describe themselves as Ford people while others see themselves as Lexus people. Aspirational purchases provide the potential for imagery among consumers, into which a brand can tap.

Another way to view consumers is by what they like to do. Are they sports nuts or ballet goers? Do they watch NASCAR or golf? By associating your brand with something that your consumer group likes or associates with can enhance your brand. It also allows you to break out from your competition.

Fruit of the Loom underwear used insight about how their consumers saw themselves to craft a campaign that stood apart from their key competitor, Hanes. Michael Jordan was Hanes's celebrity spokesperson for years and helped the company to develop a rugged yet sophisticated look for their brand. Fruit of the Loom on the other hand, had long been associated with the cute, funny, fruit guys. The trick was to make these icons relevant to their audience. The advertising agency's insight was that a large majority of Fruit of the Loom users were country music fans. They listened to country music on their iPods, watched country music performers on television, and

Figure 7.1 **Storyboard: Henry, Deluxe Boneless Box, October 2006**

Little girl puts the crusts on Henry's plate.

She then puts her egg on his plate, 'Here you go Henry, you like the white bits'.

Family look at her expectantly, 'No, Henry doesn't like boneless chicken'.

VO: The KFC Deluxe Boneless Box, eight original recipe mini breast fillets.

VO: Two regular popcorn chickens, fries, large sides, Pepsi and a choice of dips all for only £12.99.

VO: Kids won't leave a thing.

enjoyed live concerts. Based on this insight, the agency developed the "Fruit of the Loom Country Band" featuring the fruity guys. They also sponsored the Country Music Awards. By aligning their brand closely with a consumer passion, they distanced themselves from Hanes.

Usage Ritual

Most products have some form of usage ritual. Some rituals are more pronounced than others. For example, Durgee cites the rituals consumers perform when taking a shower. Some sing, some dance, and others have specific ways that they wash themselves. All of these interesting interpretations can lead to equally interesting advertising campaigns.

Observing how a consumer uses a product can provide campaign insights. Just like finding what consumers think of themselves, finding out how they use a product can be equally as engaging as research into the product or service itself. If your campaign associates your brand with consumers' usage rituals, then you can begin to make the connection between how people have come to use the brand and your campaign.

In looking at usage rituals, it is always good to assess if there is a peak moment. Is there some signature time or moment of truth that you can capitalize on? For example, when someone is seeking a loan, the moment of truth occurs during a meeting with the loan officer. This meeting can be either very good or extremely bad. Many bank advertising campaigns have been developed based on this moment in truth.

Eating popcorn is a ritualistic experience. For some people, popcorn relates to friends, family, or movies. Family movie night is the hub of the popcorn ritual. Orville Redenbacher popcorn uses this ritual to capture the beauty of family time with the brand. They associate the brand with that moment when everyone shares in the category ritual.

Rituals can become a good starting point for developing campaign ideas. When looking at usage rituals, always be aware of how advertising for this category portrays them. You may find a real hole in the marketplace that your product can occupy.

Untapped or Compelling Belief

Development of a brand begins with a problem that the brand serves to solve. Yet, as we have seen with Listerine, a brand can solve more than one problem. It can tap into an untapped or compelling belief. In Listerine's case, a simple mouthwash that kept your breath fresh and clean became a powerful germ-fighting agent that helped prevent upsetting dental visits. Having a dentist work you over is a concern for many people so Listerine really taps into an emotional core with its recent campaign and benefit.

Finding an untapped or compelling insight usually takes hard work and research. Tide discovered that moms were more concerned about their children's clothes wearing out than getting them ultra clean. This insight came from significant research. By changing Tide's focus from cleanliness to making clothes last longer, they tapped into a previously untapped belief: that every laundry detergent wears out clothes at the same rate.

Sometimes a compelling insight just happens. Take the classic case of Subway restaurants and Jared Fogle. Who would have dreamt that a college student would go on a fast food diet and lose weight? Subway's advertising agency at the time did not want to use Jared or the story. Jared and Subway prevailed and the rest is history. Now Subway is associated with healthy fare even though much of their menu is no healthier than that of any other sandwich spot.

It is not always easy to find a new approach to associate your brand with but when you do, the campaign magic begins. Finding an untapped belief is powerful stuff on which award-winning campaigns can be built.

Barrier to Using the Brand

Insights can come from looking at the barriers consumers may have for wanting to purchase a brand. That was the case with Tide where a real barrier to buying the brand was that it wasn't a good value. So what made it a good value wasn't the cost of the actual detergent itself; it was the money saved by not buying clothes as often.

Analyzing your brand's barriers can be a very fruitful exercise. It can be as simple as just listing them on a sheet of paper and then reversing them to come up with an insight. It is playing the "what if" game. What if we made clothes last longer? What if fast food was healthy? What if banks were fun? You get the idea. This type of thinking led Ogilvy & Mather to a new way of looking at an old problem. They had to figure out how to convince young men in Vietnam to wear helmets when riding motorcycles. In this IPA award-winning case, the problem that Ogilvy faced was that 97 percent of the 21 million motorcyclists in Vietnam did not wear helmets. This was a staggering percentage. Changing social behavior like this is always a real challenge.

As Ogilvy researched the problem, they found that even though most motorcyclists knew someone who had been killed or seriously injured, it did not seem to change their behavior. The other finding that research revealed was that the reasons for not wearing a helmet were trivial excuses, such as:

- It ruins my hair.
- Wearing a helmet is uncomfortable and hot.
- You look stupid wearing a helmet when no one else does.

This contrast between the awareness of the severity of the consequences and the superficiality of the excuses led to Ogilvy's creative thought: "Turn Stupid Excuses into Life Threats." The results were tremendous. Compliance to helmet wearing doubled and in some parts of Vietnam more than tripled. This is an example of a literally life-saving campaign. More than thirty-eight lives a day were saved. Now *that* is busting a barrier without busting one's head.

Category Advertising

A review of category advertising is one other approach to look for insights. There is a tendency for brands in a category to mimic each other. If someone touts that they have the best prices, you can be sure that everyone else will follow suit. Rarely does one brand let another claim a unique benefit in a category. It is always a fight to either stay one step ahead of or at least match the competition.

This also spills over to advertising. It often seems as if all advertising is the same. It is almost as if there is a formula for advertising in a given category. In an effort to be "best of class," most brands end up just a slightly shinier version of another.

This is especially true in the travel category. Just thumb through a travel magazine and look at the destinations that advertise. Imagine that you had to position a beach destination. You would likely tout the beach, fun in the sun, clear water, family fun, parties, and water sports. That is pretty much what every beach and island destination does. As we saw in Chapter 3, Fallon faced the challenge of creating a distinct position for The Bahamas.

Fallon found that all travel advertising addressed where people would like to go on vacation. So they decided to address why people wanted to go on vacation. Their research showed that regardless of the destination, nearly all consumers had trouble finding time for a vacation.

In fact, further research showed that consumers were vacation deprived. They were likely to not take all their vacation days in a given year. This led the agency team to focus on making The Bahamas synonymous with vacation rejuvenation. This idea led to the thought, "You need a vacation," which became, "You need a Bahamavention." The results were tremendous. Web site hits, vacation requests, and bookings went through the roof.

Quality of Life

In all of these examples, the account planner identifies the intersection of the brand's benefit and the quality of life it provides to the consumer. One question you can ask yourself when trying to identify an insight is, "How does this make life (of the target audience) better?" Is the message that comes out of the insight so compelling that it can make their lives better? It may seem like a tall order, but if you find the right insight it really can help the consumer to use the product or service in ways that lead to a better quality of life. — *U of Phoeniv · v can change y ur life-*

The Tide campaign convinced consumers that using the detergent would lead to better quality of life since it helped consumers save money by making clothes last longer. A Bahamas vacation led to a better quality of life by encouraging people to take a much-needed vacation. Even Fruit of the Loom products led to a better quality of life by relating their brand to the target audience's passion for country music.

Kleenex tissues also recognized the power of tapping into a quality-of-life insight. The tissue category, led by Kleenex, has long focused on product benefits such as softer tissues, more tissues in a pack, nicer looking boxes, and so on. Kleenex found through research that 70 percent of consumers dreaded getting a severe cold due to constant nose and throat irritation. While consumers wanted a soft tissue, what they really wanted was to be comforted when they felt bad. This was an emotion that Campbell's chicken noodle soup had successfully tapped into long before. Kleenex directed its efforts into becoming a "cold comfort agent," which helped the brand ward off price competition that was threatening to undermine their dominant position in the facial tissue category.

In summary, insights are all around us. The trick is to look at things in a way that is new and fresh. For seasoned account planners and advertising professionals, finding insights may seem like second nature. For inexperienced professionals and students, it may seem like a daunting task. But it just takes practice. If you take each of these approaches into finding insights, ask yourself if the brand would make someone's life better and the answer is "yes," then you know you have hit on a compelling insight.

Review Questions

1. What makes an insight?
2. How is an insight different than just information?
3. What are the types of insights?
4. What is a quality-of-life insight?

Discussion Questions

1. Do you need an insight to make an award-winning campaign?
2. How do brand positioning and brand insights differ?
3. Find a product or an ad and see if you can determine the insight that led to its development.

Additional Resources

Durgee, J. *Creative Insight: The Researcher's Art.* Chicago: Copy Workshop, 2005.
Heath, C., and D. Heath. *Made to Stick: Why Some Ideas Survive and Others Die.* New York: Random House, 2007.
Nickels, W., J. McHugh, and S. McHugh. *Understanding Business.* New York: McGraw-Hill, 2006.

Chapter 8
The Role of Advertising

Sales are down. What are you going to do to turn things around? Advertise, right? The answer is maybe yes and maybe no. While every advertising problem comes from a business problem, not every business problem is solved by advertising.

This seems to be fundamental, yet many businesses and advertising agencies assume that one leads to the other. Companies don't hire advertising agencies just to see their company's name in the media. Anyway, let's hope that isn't the case. A company hires an advertising agency because they have a business problem.

It is the account planner's role to understand what that business problem is and to determine if advertising is the best solution. It is not unlike a surgeon treating a patient. If your knee hurts, the surgeon may suggest an operation or diet to lose weight. There is no need for surgery if there is a less invasive alternative. And there is no need for advertising if there is an alternative to solving a client's problem.

One of the key aspects of any campaign is to define the role of advertising in the marketing mix. But first the business problem needs to be identified, then the marketing objectives and strategies, and then how advertising can help.

Understanding the role of advertising also focuses the account planner and the agency on what advertising can and cannot accomplish. Advertising can solve many problems but it is not a panacea. Developing an award-winning campaign begins with understanding the fundamentals of business.

Business Versus Marketing Goals

A business must make a profit to survive. From a CEO's perspective, a business must maintain a balance between revenue and expenses. Too much expense will lead to unprofitable growth. Too little revenue will lead to an unprofitable company. The CEO is constantly balancing the need for increasing the top-line growth with keeping expenses under control to maintain profit.

If the business is publicly traded, the CEO has a fiduciary responsibility to maintain value for stockholders. This means that there is a responsibility for the company to grow in value and work to increase its share price. To do so, the company must position itself for growth, generate increasing levels of profit, and seek out new growth markets.

Company's can achieve profitability, increase value for shareholders, or be responsible corporate citizens without focusing on marketing. Many companies rely on research and development as their catalysts for growth. In the short term, a CEO can reduce expenses to generate a profit. Since advertising is an aspect of marketing and marketing is but one aspect of a CEO's toolkit, it is important to understand the overall mission and vision of the company to determine what role marketing and advertising play within its overall strategy.

Yet sales and marketing can help as possible key growth areas within a company. All other functions within a company either can't grow the company or grow it in an indirect manner. For example, human resources can hire someone who helps the company to grow. But only marketing can directly impact the growth of the company.

Marketing is usually focused on areas related to market share such as brand penetration, sales, distribution, pricing, and category growth. Advertising is a means to an end within this marketing mix. Let's review advertising versus marketing goals.

The Role of Advertising Within the Marketing Mix

Traditionally, the marketing mix is known as the 4Ps: product, price, place, and promotion. In today's world, product and price are still appropriate marketing categories, but distribution replaces place and promotion is made up of integrated marketing communications that can range from advertising to short-term promotions to publicity to digital marketing (see Figure 8.1).

Before we get to advertising, let's examine the other three components of the marketing mix. Just because other components of the marketing mix may be more important than advertising doesn't mean that advertising is unnecessary. Its role may actually complement other facets of the marketing mix.

Product

The first assessment should be of the product itself. Maybe there is something about the product that is aggravating the problem. For example, suppose a

Figure 8.1   **Framework for Role of Communications within Marketing**

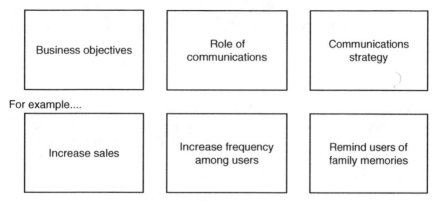

cereal brand began reducing its package size while gently increasing its price: the less-for-more theory of brand management. This strategy may seem to maximize profits, but it also may alienate consumers. Can advertising solve this problem or is a product solution necessary before advertising can be effective? However, if the product isn't aligned with current consumer values or its image is outdated, advertising can be an effective solution.

Price

The second assessment is of the price of the brand or its price/value relationship. Going back to the cereal example, if the brand has constantly increased its price while giving no more value, this is a problem that advertising may not be able to solve. Or maybe the brand has been price promoting extensively and now consumers only buy it when it is on sale. Or perhaps it is time to raise the price of the brand to keep up with rising commodity costs. These are areas where advertising can play a role. Price may be the lead but advertising can help modify the consumer's attitude toward it.

Distribution

The third assessment is of the brand's distribution. Referencing the cereal brand, it may not be carried in certain key grocery outlets or it may have lost distribution or shelf space in others. Curing this may be enough to solve the overall problem. Just like price, advertising can be a support solution for gaining distribution or recapturing lost distribution. The marketer may promise the retailer a special advertising campaign to help gain shelf space or it may offer a promotion that requires advertising. Or the problem could be as simple as the marketer giving more funds to the retailer in terms of incentives, which would render advertising unnecessary. It is pointless to advertise in markets with no distribution unless you have plans to gain distribution sometime in the near future.

Promotion

Now we are going to advertise. Not so fast. If we have run through the prior three marketing levers, we now believe that promotion is the key to solving the problem. Let's assess what types of opportunities best serve the needs of the brand. For example, you may be marketing a car that many people like but they are putting off purchasing because they are strapped for cash. This may require a short-term price incentive to get consumers into the store. Or you may be marketing a canned tomato brand that consumers love but have run out of ideas for cooking with it. In this case you might cross promote it with other complementary brands. The point is that advertising is not always the answer, even when you have run the traps on other marketing levers.

Problems That Advertising Can Solve

So we see that advertising isn't the answer to every marketing problem. Even when it might be the answer, it could be subordinate to other parts of the marketing mix. This raises the question of what advertising can do well. There are a number of areas where advertising can solve a brand's marketing problem.

Brand Awareness Generation

If people haven't heard of your brand, they are usually unlikely to buy it. Creating awareness among those who are unaware of your brand is one of the classic problems that advertising can solve. But it's not enough for people just to know your name. They must also be familiar with the benefits of the brand.

Convey New News: Inform and Educate

If you have something new to say or fresh information to impart or just want to educate consumers about how to use your brand, advertising can help you do this. This is a stepsister to awareness generation. The difference is that in this case you are probably conveying *new* news to your brand users as well as to people less familiar with your brand.

Convince Consumers to Try the Brand

Advertising can be a persuasive tool for getting consumers to try something new. It is not the only method, of course. You could hand samples out on the street corner, for example. But advertising incentives or other approaches can be effective at convincing a consumer to try a brand. An ancillary benefit of this solution is to remind consumers to either buy or use the brand. This is a mainstay of consumer packaged-goods advertising.

Change Consumer Attitudes Toward a Brand

If consumers have a belief about the brand that you want to change, then advertising is certainly the best solution. The problem may be that consumers feel your brand is dated or irrelevant. Or it might be that they believe that the brand isn't a good value. Whatever the consumer mind-set, advertising done right can change consumer attitudes toward a brand.

Associate the Brand with an Image

One of the key aspects of a brand is the emotional connection to it. Advertising can tap into that emotional connection by accessing a consumer's need state. Just think about any liquor or fashion brands. The brand is highly identified with an image and advertising can reinforce that association. The ultimate goal of advertising is to add value to the brand. The brand icon era of the 1970s showed how advertising could add value to brands with characters such as Charlie the Tuna, the Jolly Green Giant, and the Marlboro Man. This continues in today's advertising. A great example of contemporary advertising is Geico's various campaigns. The gecko and cavemen are two very popular icons. These icons set a brand apart. The advertising is as unique as the product.

The Influence of Advertising

The role advertising plays in a campaign generally fall into these five big categories: generating brand awareness, conveying new news, convincing consumers to try the brand, changing consumer attitudes toward a brand, and associating the brand with an image.

A problem that advertising can solve may be a combination any of these five categories. A new brand obviously requires awareness but also may need to carve out a niche in the market so that its brand image is unique. Mature brands may just require changing attitudes toward it. An example of the latter is the current advertising war between Microsoft and Apple. Apple has long painted its brand as associated with the creative set and has cast all personal computers using Microsoft's operating system as brands for more analytical thought. The classic Apple vs. PC campaign carries this out brilliantly.

However, Microsoft fought back with its own campaign. It is based on the following sets of objectives:

- Business objective: To increase the penetration of personal computers, which will increase sales of Microsoft software
- Marketing objective: To increase brand penetration by convincing consumers that personal computers meet more than just functional needs
- Role advertising plays: To convince consumers that personal computers meet more than functional needs by associating PCs with a creative class of consumer

The role advertising plays in the marketing mix is tied directly to the marketing objective, which is tied directly to the business objective. By working through the stages—the business problem, to marketing strategy, to the role that advertising plays within the marketing context—you will have a clear focus on what the advertising must accomplish.

Measuring the Contribution of Advertising

Establishing the role of advertising within the marketing mix is one thing; measuring it is quite another. In Chapter 16, we will discuss measuring all aspects of advertising. Here we will discuss the overall aspects of measurement.

Measuring the impact of advertising on consumer behavior is pretty simple. If the role of advertising is to make people aware of your brand, they either become aware of it or don't. However, measuring the business impact of advertising is another matter. Just because a consumer is aware of your brand, did they buy it? And was it the advertising that contributed to that sale or was it other factors? The old quotation attributed to John Wanamaker, founder of the first department store in the United States, "Half my advertising is wasted; the trouble is I don't know which half" still rings true.

So, the big challenge in measuring the role of advertising is not necessarily whether the advertising did its job, but if that job actually means something to the success of the business side of the brand. In other words, how did the advertising contribute to the sales of the brand?

The IPA case studies do a marvelous job of isolating the impact of advertising and its ultimate contribution to the brand's business. It is the rigorous nature of these case studies that sets them apart from other advertising cases in the field.

One example is a case study of a KFC campaign in the United Kingdom. In the assessment of the impact of advertising for this brand, they sought to demonstrate advertising's impact in three ways:

1. By demonstrating that the role of advertising worked
2. By quantifying and/or eliminating all other variables that may have contributed to the success of sales by the brand during which time the advertising had run
3. By using a sophisticated econometric model to quantify the contribution that advertising made to sales over that period

The roles that advertising played in the KFC campaign included:

- To create food desire
- To evoke a new sympathy with families
- To prompt craving for KFC among a youth audience

The way they measured this was to measure the perceptions of KFC's food versus its competition to see if it impacted a measure of "delicious-tasting food." To measure whether they evoked sympathy with families they asked mom if they agreed that "the advertising is for people like me." And to measure whether they successfully prompted craving among the youth market, they measured whether consumers thought that "KFC has something new and different to offer." All of these measurements, which showed positive results, show how the advertising worked and suggest that the advertising has motivated consumers to take action.

However, the trick is that other aspects of the marketing mix could have provided a stronger inducement for sales than advertising. In this case, the agency team went through a methodical analysis of what other variables could have impacted the success of this campaign.

To do this, the agency team analyzed variables from the brand itself, the competition, and the consumer's environment. The following is an abbreviated list of variables that were analyzed in each of these three areas.

1. KFC Brand

The agency assessed the following questions regarding the brand.

- Was there a change to the food quality or taste that would impact the brand?
- Was there a new product that would impact perception?
- Was there a price difference that caused a change?
- Was there an operational change in the stores such as longer hours, more stores, cleaner stores, etc., that improved perception of the brand?
- Was the change just a function of media spending?

The answer to all of these questions was no. So, they were eliminated as variables that could have impacted the business and/or communication scores.

2. Competition

The same rigor in looking at the brand was applied to the competition. Here are some of the questions that were analyzed.

- Was KFC the beneficiary of a decline in a competitor's perception?
- Did the competition raise prices and therefore impact KFC's price perception?
- Did the competition decrease their advertising spending during this period of time?

The answer to these questions was also no. Again, the group began to eliminate other possible causes.

3. Consumer

The last category was analyzing consumer perceptions and environment to see if there were external factors at play.

- Did chicken become more popular in general, which could have raised KFC's business?
- Was there a socioeconomic answer to the increase in sales?
- Was the consumer less concerned about healthy eating during this time?

Again, the answers to this and the other questions was a resounding no.

Based on this analysis, the team then developed an econometric model that was used to quantify the effects of advertising on the business. This model looks at the incremental sales generated by advertising during this timeframe and compares it to the advertising dollar allocation to determine a return on investment. In the case of KFC, the return on investment was $4.63 for every $1.00 spent on advertising. No wonder it is an IPA case.

It is impossible for a student campaign to be this rigorous about measurement since NSAC campaigns are theoretical and IPA campaigns are actually done in the marketplace. However, it is important to understand how you can begin to link the role that advertising plays in the marketing mix to the overall business.

In summary, advertising is a part of the marketing mix and ultimately is used as a tool to solve a business problem. To do a proper advertising campaign, you must understand what role advertising plays within the marketing mix. Once this is defined, then you can apply stringent criteria to measuring the impact that advertising has on those goals. By systematically isolating advertising as the variable that impacts business, it is possible to generate a specific return on investment.

Review Questions

1. What is a marketing objective?
2. How do business objectives and marketing objectives interrelate?
3. How does a marketing objective differ from an advertising objective?
4. What are the roles that advertising plays within a marketing mix?
5. How do you isolate the impact of advertising's contribution to business objectives?

Discussion Questions

1. What are examples of advertising campaigns where the role is clearly defined? What are examples where it is not clear?
2. Should you develop an advertising campaign prior to clearly defining the role of advertising?
3. How should advertising be measured? Can its impact really be calculated?

Additional Resources

Aaker, D., and A. Biel, eds. *Brand Equity and Advertising: Advertising's Role in Building Strong Brands.* Hillsdale, NJ: Lawrence Erlbaum, 1993.
Jugenheimer, D., & Kelley, L. *Advertising Management.* Armonk, NY: M.E. Sharpe, 2009.

Chapter 9

Segmenting the Target Market

The most important aspect of the account planner's role in developing an award-winning campaign is the ability to determine the target audience for marketing efforts. Understanding who the consumers are, how frequently they buy your brand, and why they buy your brand provides a framework for segmenting your target market. Wrap this understanding in the context of overall consumer values and you can define your market from a marketing and then from a more detailed advertising perspective.

As you help craft a strategy for market segmentation, there needs to be a balance between the marketing goals and the need for advertising input. From a marketing perspective, it is crucial to define a market in terms of size of the opportunity along with the purchase dynamics. From an advertising perspective, it is important to understand who the consumer is, how the brand fits into his or her life, and how their environment has contributed to his or her personality.

Marketing Understanding

Every brand wants to grow. Whether it is getting more people to drink Coke, buy their insurance from State Farm, or use Yahoo! as their Internet portal, all companies want to increase their sales and brand penetration. Even if you are marketing a cause, such as Stop Teenage Smoking, the goal is for someone to do something.

The manner in which a brand decides to grow strategically has a marked impact on what they target. And there are limited options for how a brand can grow:

- Increase the amount that current users purchase.
- Increase the number of new users of the brand.
- Switch users from a competing brand.
- Increase the number of users in the category.

All of these are viable ways to grow a brand. However, each has pros and cons.

The first way to grow your brand is to get people who already like your brand to buy more of it. It seems logical enough. If someone already likes the brand, it probably isn't all that tough to get them to "do it one more time." Many brands focus their attention on their most loyal customers since they may represent a disproportionate amount of the brand's sales. The argument for this strategy is that a small incremental gain in purchase frequency can mean big sales dollars in return. That has led many brands to develop loyalty programs—from airlines to grocery stores to online retailers—all in the quest to maximize their sales. The fallacy of this strategy is that by focusing attention on who is currently buying your brand, you could be setting yourself up for not replenishing your customer base. Increasing the frequency of purchase among your current target market could mask the problem of fewer people buying your brand. As loyal users eventually leave, you are left with no one to replace them.

That leads to how you can increase the market penetration of the brand. For most brands, there is a point where a consumer begins to show interest in or needs your good or service. In the case of auto insurance, it is the moment an individual can get a driver's license. In the case of diapers, it is when someone has a baby. If you are selling computers, it is when a new business is established or an existing business expands. All of these moments create an opportunity for a brand to target those who are entering the category for the first time. You want to attract these new users before they have a chance to fall in love with a competing brand. This is why many brands spend their resources cultivating the youth market. They hope to get consumers to adopt their brand at an early age so that they will stay with them for a long time.

Another option is to increase the penetration level of a certain demographic group that is currently under-represented in your customer base. For example, Latinos are a high-growth demographic group. You may identify this group and others as key growth audiences for the future of the brand.

Another way to increase a brand's penetration is to sell additional products or services to the same client. This is particularly true in the case of business-to-business marketing. For example, if you are the marketing director for Dell computers, you may use your relationship with a customer's IT (informational technology) department to sell servers, laptops, and even a service agreement. The same concept is true in the financial services industry. Once an individual opens an account, the institution may work to provide savings programs, mutual funds, loans, and insurance. It is that one-stop shopping idea.

Another way to gain new users is to add users of competing brands to your customer base. This is certainly the case in mature categories such as cellular phone providers or packaged-goods categories such as laundry detergent. This is a common marketing strategy in the United States with so many categories at a mature stage in their product life cycle. This strategy is sometimes the only way to grow but it comes at a price. In essence, you are asking someone to give up a relationship to come to you. Unless your brand has a compelling benefit, many times this can turn into a promotional slugfest. A discount or price war may ensue in which neither side wins.

Another method for increasing penetration is to increase the pie or expand the category. This is a strategy employed by a category leader to grow their brand. One method within this framework is to reach out to traditional nonusers of the category. For example, senior citizens may not be the traditional market for downloading rap music. However, if you can convince grandparents that they could be closer to their grandchildren by giving them a gift card to download the kids' favorite rap music, you could expand the number of people in that category.

Before segmenting the target, it is important to understand how the brand will grow. This is the key to developing the marketing and advertising targets. The first step in defining the target is to understand who buys the brand.

Who Is Buying My Brand?

It may seem rather obvious that you should know who is buying your product or service. If you are selling a new technology to the oil industry, you might actually know your customer, the chief buyer, by first name. However, if you are selling a one-dollar can of beans, you have millions of customers. Regardless of the size of your market and audience, you need to begin with some fundamentals.

Figure 9.1 is a graphic representation of the stages of segmentation: (1) How many people there are in your market. If you are selling to the oil industry, there may be only 20 companies that have a need for your service. If you are marketing to adults aged 18 to 24, there are 28.5 million of them in the United States. (2) Who is actually buying the brand? (3) How do they go about making a purchase? (4) Why do they buy? (5) What is their relationship to the brand?

The initial stages are descriptive of who the target is while the latter are more descriptive of how you might view them if you were to carry on a conversation with them. Ultimately, when you are segmenting a target market to deliver advertising, you understand who you are communicating with.

The key is to understand the foundation of the marketplace. The essential

Figure 9.1   **Segmentation Pyramid**

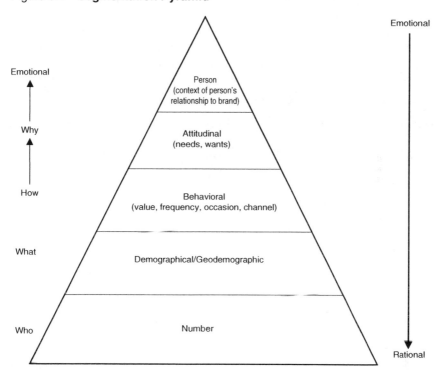

factor might be the total number of people in a specific demographic or the total number of people buying your brand or others in your category. The first step to understanding a market is to get a feel for the magnitude of the audience.

Counting the number of people in a market can be an easy task in a business-to-business situation: just a matter of adding up the number of contracts. If you are selling a product to a grocery chain, you will need a list of transactions and if you are selling online, you will need to know the number of individual ISP addresses.

All of this information is necessary to understand your target market.

What Do You Know About Them?

Now that you know *who* is buying your brand, what do you know about them? A good place to start is to understand the demographics. Is your audience made up of men or women? College educated or just high school grads? Affluent or poor? Is there a significant ethnic mix or age group? All of this information can be gathered from your customers. There are syndicated research studies such

Figure 9.2   **Claritas Information**

Upper Crust

Wealthy, Older, without Kids

The nation's most exclusive address, Upper Crust, is the location of the wealthiest lifestyle in America—a haven for empty-nesting couples between the ages of 45 and 64. No segment has a higher concentration of residents earning more than $100,000 a year or possessing a postgraduate degree. And none has a more opulent standard of living.

Social Group: Elite Suburbs

Lifestage Group: Affluent Empty Nests

2008 Statistics:
U.S. households: 1,742,531 (1.52%)
Median HH income: $114,343

Lifestyle Traits:
- Shop at Saks Fifth Ave.
- Spend $3,000+ on foreign travel
- Read *Washington Post*
- Watch Golf Channel
- Aston Martin DB9

Demographics Traits:

Urbanicity: Suburban

Income: Wealthy

Income Producing-
Assets: Elite

Age Range: 45–64

Presence of Kids: HH w/o Kids

Homeowner ship: Mostly owners

Employment levels: Management

Education levels: Graduate Plus

Ethnic diversity: White, Asian, Mixed

as MRI (Mediamark Research and Intelligence) and SMRB (an abbreviation that now refers to Experian Simmons syndicated research) that can provide this information and much more. Or you can do your own research and find out the fundamental demographic makeup of your target market.

Since much of today's information about sales and customers contains a person's name, address, phone number, and e-mail address, there is also a wealth of data that can be appended to these customer records to add significant dimension to the person buying your brand. The Claritas company is the leader in this field. If you provide customer transactional records to them they will provide a geodemographic analysis of your customer database. This will include a variety of demographic and geographic variables that can offer a robust way to look at your customers.

Figure 9.2 shows the type of information that Claritas can provide. Much of this information is used in marketing and media planning since media habits are one of the data-appended resources available from Claritas.

One of the key points of analysis at this stage of segmentation is whether consumers buying your brand are similar to those who purchase other brands in the same category. For example, suppose that the majority of your buyers more than 45 years of age, yet the category overall appeals to younger

Figure 9.3   **Purchaser/User/Influencer Triangle**

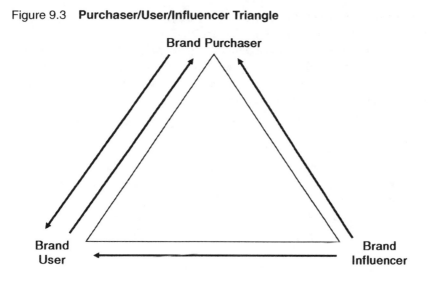

people. That would suggest that there is an opportunity for your brand to gain younger users. Or you might conduct research to understand why younger users are not attracted to your brand.

Once you understand who is buying your brand, you can then begin to understand the dynamics of the user.

Target Triangle

It is obvious that a key target segment is people who buy the product. These people are called brand purchasers. However, a brand purchaser may not be the only person or even the best person to influence with advertising. They may not be the person who is actually consuming the brand. There are numerous consumer packaged-good examples of this dynamic, such as when Mom buys cereal, canned pasta, cookies, or chips for her children. The child may not only be the user of the brand but, depending upon how much influence he has or the amount of whining she does, the child may direct mom to buy a particular brand. This second person in the so-called target triangle is the brand user.

In the business-to-business arena, there are also many cases in which the purchaser of a good or service may not be the person actually using it. The chief financial officer (CFO) may arrange for a deal with FedEx to ship all the company's packages, but the administrative assistant or mailroom clerk may the one using the service. They may be able to influence the CFO's decision. In many cases, however, the brand user and brand purchaser are one in the individual.

The third person in the target triangle is the purchase influencer. A purchase influencer is someone who does not buy the brand or use it, but has heavy sway over the person who does. For example, a father may influence the purchase of an automobile for his grown daughter. She may consult him as to the most reliable car or dealership. She will ultimately make the purchase but her father helps direct the purchase. We often see purchase influencers in where large ticket items are concerned and expertise is required to make a purchase. A good example of this is the purchase of a surround-sound stereo system.

The role of a purchase influencer is particularly strong in business-to-business purchases. The purchase of IT equipment or software will likely be influenced by a number of people: those who use it on a daily basis, those who maintain it, and those who make the purchase and negotiate the service agreements. The purchase influencers might range from someone with deep technical skill to someone who isn't comfortable at all with technology. That is why brands flourish in this environment. A well-known brand such as IBM can make everyone feel comfortable.

As the account planner, you must understand the various roles within the target triangle (see Figure 9.3). Each brand or company will have a unique set of purchasers, users, and/or influencers. Some purchases are very straightforward while others are more complex. Some may involve one aspect of the triangle and others may involve all three. Regardless, it is up to you to understand the various roles and how they might impact your ultimate target segmentation decisions.

How Are They Buying Your Brand?

Many marketers define their target market based on usage, a behavioral measure of how frequently someone buys a brand. There are secondary resources and electronic point-of-sale information services that help identify various stages of usage. The fundamentals of usage are to look at heavy, medium, and light users of your brand with heavy being the most frequent usage and light the least. For example, if you were defining usage for Budweiser beer, you might segment the audience based on usage as follows.

- Noncategory user: consumer who does not drink beer but may drink other alcoholic beverages or none at all
- Category user but not brand user: consumers who drink beer but don't drink Budweiser
- Light user: Budweiser user who buys a six-pack about once every three months
- Medium user: Budweiser user who buys a six-pack about once a month
- Heavy user: Budweiser user who buys at least one six-pack every week

The Pareto principle, named for Italian economist Vilfredo Pareto, states that 20 percent of consumers represent 80 percent of the usage or purchases of a brand. While this 80/20 rule may or may not be exactly what your brand or category purchase dynamics are, there is typically some form of heavy usage component.

Obviously, retaining your heavy users is a crucial aspect of your brand's survival. The loss of one heavy user may require you to add sixteen new users just to make up for the lost volume. That can be a pretty scary prospect, which is why many companies devote significant resources to frequent user programs. The airline industry is a great example of this concept.

However, many brands focus on their heavy users to the detriment of adding new users to the brand. While retaining heavy users is important, they don't add volume to the brand since they are likely consuming as much as they possibly can. And without adding new users to your brand, you are risking long-term failure.

Rather than focusing on the heavy user segment, marketing should concentrate on purchasers who use your product less frequently or who may be in the category but do not purchase your brand.

Another way of looking at behavior is to analyze when or where people are purchasing the brand. A fast food restaurant might segment its market based on when they eat. The segmentation strategy would be based on mealtimes. If you are marketing a soft drink such as Coke, you may analyze where consumers buy the brand. Are they buying it at the grocery store, at a convenience store, at the drugstore, or in a vending machine on campus? Each of these venues may have different types of customers and will require different types of marketing and advertising approaches.

As the account planner, you can use these behavioral measurements to craft a segmentation strategy for any brand. The key is to analyze both the brand and the category to understand the strengths and weaknesses. Behavioral targeting can be a very good approach to market segmentation

Why Are They Buying?

Up until now, we have discussed segmentation by describing the consumer's state of being. Whether it is demographically who they are or behaviorally how they buy, these are all factors that describe the consumer's state of being. However, to get to the heart of the market you need to understand the consumer's state of mind. *Why* are they buying your brand? What emotional need does it fulfill?

To develop compelling advertising, you really need to understand the various need states that categories and brands fulfill. A need state is defined by a group of consumers who are alike in the terms of how a brand fits into their lives. Categories and the brands that make them up fit various need states within the consumer spectrum. If they didn't, why would there be so many different beer brands or water brands or automobiles and trucks? At a functional level, these brands do the same thing. They either quench your thirst or get you from point A to point B. We all know that there is more to life than just the fundamentals and that is where brands fill an emotional niche.

Let's examine the need states of college male beer drinkers. One need state is "I want to get drunk as cheaply as possible." I am sure that you can think of brands of beer that you would associate with this. A common need state is "I want to be one of the guys." Budweiser has built their franchise on filling this need state. Their beer is all about rewarding hard work, heritage, and being together. "This Bud's for you," symbolizes the sense of being asked to be a part of the group. Another need state might be, "I want to be perceived as cool." The current advertising campaign for Dos Equis, "The most interesting man in the world," fits this need state to a tee. It associates a mysterious man with the brand and through that association indicates that if you drink this beer, you will be seen as "cool."

The need state will ultimately allow you to create a target market that is more personal in nature. For example, if you were marketing tires, you may have the need state of safety or the need state of power and performance. Michelin is positioned for "safety conscious parents" while Pirelli is positioned for "performance seekers." They market to totally different need states with fundamentally the same product.

Who Are They?

You may know how and why people buy your brand, but what do you know about their personalities? What are their needs and wants? Once you understand the need state that your brand fulfills, what other things make your targets unique? More importantly, what do you know about your consumers that might give you leverage when communicating with them?

One way to understand the individuals in your target market is by looking at their interests and lifestyle. For example, if you knew that your beer-drinking audience was a bunch of party animals it might influence how you speak to them. Conversely, if you knew that they were seeking art and cultural knowledge you might need to approach them differently.

There are many syndicated research studies such as SMRB and MRI that offer information about a target market. Items such as the media they consume, the events they attend, or even the other goods and services they buy can all help to paint a picture of your target market.

The more you can add a personal dimension to your target market, the better your advertising will be.

What Has Influenced Them?

Another feature of the target audience is what generation they belong to. Different generations look at the world through different eyes and experiences. There is a considerable body of research regarding differences between generations. Typically, a generation defines a common group based on when they were born. Each generation spans about 20 years.

Historically, generations have been very accurate in predicting future behavior. It is not that everyone is a clone within that age range but they do share common values. For example, baby boomers, the generation born between 1946 and 1964, are characterized as being unapologetic consumers who put work first. They tend to be control freaks and have been described as forever young. They were impacted greatly by the Vietnam War, the assassination of President John F. Kennedy, the music festival at Woodstock, the first moon landing, the Beatles, and the civil rights movement.

There is quite a contrast between baby boomers and the generation that followed them, Generation X, which is people born between 1965 and 1977. This group is characterized as fiercely individualistic, skeptical, media savvy, and wanting a blend of work and family. They were impacted by the Watergate scandal, the tearing down of the Berlin Wall, the dotcom boom and bust, and being the first children of working mothers.

You can see how these two groups may have wildly different points of view. The current generation, Generation Y or the millennial generation, born between 1978 and 1995, is characterized as multicultural, group oriented, tech savvy, self-entitled, and highly connective. Their defining moments have included the introduction of social media such as Facebook and MySpace, the introduction of the iPod, 9/11, the Iraq War, and the election of the first African American president.

Understanding the context of the target market is crucial to being able to communicate with these groups. As you paint a picture of the target market, it is important to understand their life journey.

Segmenting the Target

Now it is time to segment your market. As we have said, you can do it demographically, behaviorally, and by need state. All of these methods are viable ways of looking at the target market.

Figure 9.4 shows a student method of segmenting the 13- to 24-year-

Figure 9.4   **Segmenting the Target**

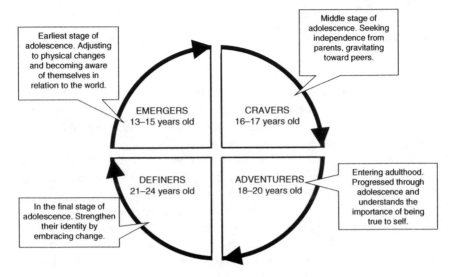

old age group. As you can see, the creators have separated the group into four segments, naming and describing each one. The only thing missing is quantifying how many people would be in each segment.

However, this is a good example of the way universities segment a market for the NSAC competition. Every award-winning NSAC campaign is characterized by a well-crafted segmentation of the target market.

Figure 9.5 shows an example of a chicken fast food restaurant segmentation that describes each segment and also offers the percent of usage for each one. In this case, the goal of the brand was to understand the category of those consumers who eat chicken at fast food restaurants. You can see that in this case, there are consumers who eat chicken at fast food restaurants but not at chicken fast food restaurants. This makes up 20 percent of the market, so it is significant. The largest segment is chicken cravers followed by the value conscious and family feeders. There is a small segment that picks up chicken for special occasions such as picnics.

In addition to segmenting the market it is important to recommend which segment you believe has the most potential for your brand. Once you have pinpointed the specific target segment, you are ready to personify it.

Personifying the Target

You should constantly work to humanize the target market. The first step is to give the entire segment a name, such as "emergers" or "cravers," as

Figure 9.5   **Chicken QSR Segmentation**

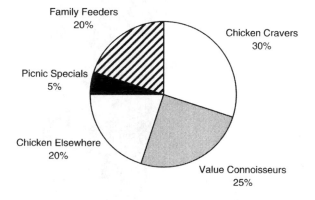

illustrated in Figure 9.4. But you still need to put a face to the name, or personify the target. It is important for the brand group and the creative group to have a single target in mind when developing a campaign. Any effective piece of communication should be written at a personal level.

Figure 9.6 shows an example for the "emerger" segment, Andrew Walters. In this approach, the student NSAC team created a consumer narrative, a brief story about the target with the goal of bringing it to life. Creating a story about the consumer is one way to connect the consumer to the creative and brand group.

In their book *Creating Brand Loyalty,* Richard Czerniawski and Michael Maloney do an excellent job of discussing how to define a target market and bring it down to a personal level. Figure 9.7 is an example of the Tide target segment from their book. From this example, you can see that Mary Beth Williams is a very busy mother. She is taking care of the kids and her husband and seems to be constantly looking for ways to save dollars. You get a real sense of what Mary Beth is like and how to communicate with her.

Often advertising agencies and NSAC college teams will develop short videos that capture the essence of the target audience. Usually no more than a minute in length, these so-called targeting videos work to capture the emotional life of the target, which you can't always get from reading a simple description.

Summary

One of the key elements to developing an award-winning campaign is to properly segment your market. Great care should be taken when selecting a target and determining why you should target them. It is crucial to move beyond

Figure 9.6 **Emerger Target Market Profile**

EMERGER TARGET MARKET PROFILE

Andrew Walters

Andrew is 14 years old, and a freshman at St. Charles East High School in St. Charles, Illinois. New to the high school scene, Andrew idolizes his 17 year old brother Brian, taking social cues from the example he sets. Since Brian is one of the most popular kids in school, Andrew is insecure about his ability to follow in his brother's footsteps. Everyday after school Andrew and his friends walk to the local pizza place, where they play video games and hang out. On the way home, Andrew likes to listen to his favorite radio station, KISS FM, where he jams out to the latest hits from his mom's SUV. As a reward for helping around the house, Andrew's parents let him surf the web for a few hours before doing his homework. He often checks out his friend's MySpace profiles, commenting on their pictures and updating his top friends.

Network Cable TV
Leisure Time:
MTV, Cartoon Network, Nickelodeon

Non-Traditional
Out-of-Home Entertainment:
Movie Teasers

Internet
Homework Tool & Social Community:
Neopets, Facebook, YouTube, ESPN, MSN, AOL, Yahoo!, Google

Radio
Pop-Culture Requirement:
Contemporary Hit Music

Outdoor
Do You Go2gospum:
Kid Points

Figure 9.7   **Target Customer Profile, Tide Retail Consumer Example**

Name: Mary Beth Williams
Gender: Female   Age: 38
Marital status (married to/number of years):   John (8)–2nd marriage
Children (ages):   Tricia (17), Billy (15), John Jr. (18), James (15), Melissa (6), Rob and Ed (4)

Occupation	Full-time caretaker, part-time bookkeeper for husband John's roofing business
Education	Regina High School
Personal auto	Ford Bronco
Currently working on	Picking up after children!
My favorite leisure activity is	I don't have time for leisure
I stay home to watch (on TV)	"Rosanne," "Home Improvement," "As the World Turns"
Last good book I read	I don't have time to read books!
The newspaper/magazines I usually read include	*People, Readers Digest, Good Housekeeping, Enquirer*
My favorite music/performer is	Classic Rock (The Eagles)
The last vacation I took was	Last summer we drove to and camped in Yosemite
I love to shop for	Earrings
My favorite shopping place is	Flea markets and garage sales
What my friends say about me (when I'm not in their presence) is	If she doesn't slow down she is going to drive herself into the ground
If I could change one thing about myself it would be	I would have gone to college
A really good evening to me is	Go out alone with John to either a movie or dinner (just get away from the house and kids)
My dream life is	To win the lottery and not have to do a damn thing
The reason(s) I choose Tide (vs. competitive brands) is	Tide gets even the dirtiest clothes clean (and I can tell you my husband and the twins really get their clothes dirty) without damaging the fabric so we can all look our best. Also, I can usually buy it on special.

demographic and behavioral descriptions of the target. While they provide the foundation they do not supply the reason the target makes a purchase or the context behind the target. To get to these aspects of the target, you must understand their need state and the values that surround their decisions. Once you segment the target, then you should bring that segment to life through a consumer narrative, whether in written form or in a short video. By doing this, you have a good chance of creating an award-winning campaign.

Review Questions

1. What are the various methods that you can use to segment a target market?
2. What are the limitations of demographic variables for segmenting a target market?
3. What is the difference between targeting behaviorally versus a need state?
4. What kinds of problems might you encounter when trying to collect consumer information?
5. How is selling to an individual different from selling to a group?

Discussion Questions

1. What are the different roles in the purchase process and how might they change as a brand matures?
2. What type of segmentation makes for the best advertising?
3. What are the advantages and disadvantages of each of the three ways a company can increase sales using segmentation strategy: increase usage, add more users, or get users to switch to your brand?
4. How important are generational differences in segmenting a target market?

Additional Resources

Cahill, D. *Lifestyle Market Segmentation.* Binghamton, NY: Haworth, 2005.
McDonald, M., and A. Dunbar. *Market Segmentation: How to Do It, How to Profit from It.* Maryland Heights, MO: Elsevier Science, 2004.
Treacy, M., and F. Wiersema. *The Discipline of Market Leaders: Choose Your Customers, Narrow Your Focus, Dominate Your Market.* Jackson, TN: Perseus, 1997.

Chapter 10
Brand Positioning

How you position your brand in a crowded marketplace is what separates brands that rise to the top from brands that sink into mediocrity. Regardless of whether you are developing a global brand campaign or are competing in a student advertising competition, understanding and applying the principals of brand positioning are crucial to your success.

To position a brand, you need to understand your target market inside and out. You must be able to translate the brand's attributes into consumer benefits that hit an emotional hot button. You need to understand the brand's personality and how it may differ from others in the category. All of these elements combine to make up a brand position.

As an account planner, it is your job to make sure the brand is properly positioned. If you are working with a packaged-goods manufacturer, you might work with in-house brand managers on this task. If you are working with a retailer or a business-to-business marketer or are a student participating in the NSAC competition, then this task may rest solely on your shoulders.

Regardless of the situation, you must know the tenets of brand positioning to move any company forward. It is the cornerstone of all marketing and communications efforts.

Classic Brand Positioning

Figure 10.1 is a brand positioning format that originated from Procter & Gamble, which is credited with the development of brand management practices adopted by many other companies. This brand positioning format is one of the universally adopted practices for uniquely positioning a brand in the marketplace. By looking at each aspect of the brand positioning format, your goal is to create a unique position for your brand in the marketplace.

While the elements of the brand position look basic enough, it is the in-

Figure 10.1 **Brand Positioning Statement**

Brand Positioning Statement
To _____, _____ is the brand of
(target market)   (brand)
_____ that _____
(competitive framework)   (benefit)
because _____
(reason why)
The brand personality is _____
_____

teraction that makes this format a powerful tool. Let's look at the elements and how they interact with each other.

The first item in the brand positioning statement is the target market definition. As you recall from Chapter 9, this is where you apply the principals of the conceptual target audience definition. The target definition of the positioning statement must be more than just a demographic definition. It must contain the target market's mind-set or motivation. For example, it is not enough to say, "Moms with kids" for a food brand. You must paint a better picture of whom you are targeting. This might be "penny-pinching moms" or "single urban moms" or "suburban soccer moms." To gain a successful brand position, you must define the target in a specific way that helps to position your brand differently than others in the market.

The second aspect of the brand positioning statement is the frame of reference. This is who the brand competes against or what category they are in. Defining the competitive frame of reference may sound pretty easy. If you are marketing Coke, isn't your competitive frame of reference other soft drinks? It could be. Or it could be anything that a consumer drinks to quench their thirst, including water. Or if you are marketing Mountain Dew, your frame of reference could be anything that provides a boost in energy including energy drinks and coffee. So, even though the frame of reference is typically cut and dried, it is important to think it through. If you change the competitive frame of reference, you may impact the subsequent brand benefits your product delivers to the market.

Here are two ways to assess the frame of reference. The first is the current business aspect of the brand. Whom must the brand compete against to gain market share? This indicates where the brand is today. The second is who you want to compete against in the future. Who do you want to beat? At this point you are checking for vulnerabilities in the market. For example, Lexus positioned itself against much more expensive luxury automobiles since it believed that it could gain a much larger market share from this comparison than by being the top-of-the-line midsized sedan.

Over time, the competitive frame of reference may change or expand as the brand changes or the category expands. If you are selling pudding, your initial frame of reference might be all other puddings. Over time, you may want to expand your thinking to all desserts. You could expand this thinking to add after-school snacks. Sometimes, to grow your brand you need to expand your sights, which can then change the dynamics of the positioning statement.

The third part of the brand positioning statement is the consumer benefit. What is the intended consumer "take-away"? An example could be toothpaste that whitens teeth while it cleans. Or it could be a brand of detergent that is fast acting or a deodorant that is long lasting. The secret to the brand benefit is to be as precise as possible. You can't be wishy-washy or obtuse in your language. Clear, matter-of-fact writing is in order here.

Another potential pitfall when developing the brand benefit is that it might not be a meaningful point of difference. The benefit must be both compelling and unique. It is not enough for toothpaste to whiten teeth and freshen breath. That indeed may be a benefit, but every toothpaste on the market can make this claim. The price of entry into the marketplace, what it costs a competitor to compete in a certain market category, can be a unique benefit for your brand.

The benefit should be so distinctive that you cannot substitute another brand in the positioning statement. The more commodity-like the brand is, the more difficult the task of developing a meaningful point of difference. This is particularly true of developing a functional point of difference as in the toothpaste example. The benefit may have to be of a more emotional nature or feeling. This can be difficult to accomplish but if your brand captures the emotional territory first then it can be in a unique position.

The fourth aspect of the brand positioning statement is the rationale. This is the support for the benefit. It is the explanation of the product or brand attributes that provide the benefit to the consumer. For example, if your toothpaste whitens teeth better than any other toothpaste, the reason may be a special new formula that combines a whitening agent with a cleaning agent. The explanation is fact based and not mere puffery. As the account planner, you must ensure that the facts are there and that they are compelling. Eventually, the reasons to believe may become a part of an advertising campaign, so discovering the rationale is crucial to the success of the brand and future advertising.

For consumers, the reason why must be understandable as well as believable. Just because a car comes with a gyroscope that adjusts steering to automatically aim the car on the highway doesn't mean the average person will understand it or care. If the same navigational device is used on space capsules, then a consumer might see that there is a pretty special reason to believe. This underscores the point that when writing a positioning statement, you need to write in clear consumer-friendly language. This should not be a technical analysis even though you may have technical reasons why your brand performs the way it does. This is where an account planner can help a brand manager craft the statement so that it makes business sense as well as consumer sense.

The final aspect of the brand positioning statement is the brand's personality. The brand personality is used in a number of ways. It is important in establishing what voice the advertising might use. For example, there is a big difference between being wholesome and being irreverent. That may sum up one of the big differences between McDonald's and Burger King. Brand personality also can take on strategic value. This is particularly true in categories such as liquor where imagery is one of the crucial differences that separate one brand from another.

Now that you have read about all aspects of brand positioning, take a look at the example in Figure 10.2. This sums up the classic brand positioning work in clear Procter & Gamble (P&G) fashion.

Contemporary Brand Positioning

The classic brand positioning statement serves the consumer packaged-goods business very well. However, many brands use an abbreviated version of the classic statement to assess their own position in the marketplace. The following are a couple of examples of well-known brands and their positioning.

- Motel 6: "To frugal people, Motel 6 is the alternative to staying with family and friends that provides a welcoming, comfortable night's rest at a reasonable price."
- Target: "To value conscious consumers of all income levels, Target is the brand of discount retailer that delivers contemporary clothes and accessories at a reasonable price."

Figure 10.2   **Brand Positioning Statement Example**

For *cost-conscious moms of large blue-collar families with active children*, Tide is the brand of laundry detergent that *gets clothes their cleanest and keeps them looking new* because "improved" Tide formulation powers out stains while keeping clothes from fading and fraying.

The brand personality is dependable, strong, practical, and traditional.

The interesting item in the first example is the frame of reference. You might suspect that the frame of reference would be other hotels and motels. But in their positioning, it is actually staying at a friend's home. So the test of the positioning is the comfort level of Motel 6. Is it as comfortable as or more comfortable than staying with on a sofa or in a guest room of a friend's house? We hope that the answer is yes.

Everyone knows that Target offers fashion-forward merchandise at a reasonable price. This is reflected in their positioning statement. The interesting aspect of their positioning statement is that they define their audience as "value conscious shoppers of all income levels." So the target market is a mind-set rather than a specific income level.

Each of these examples is an abbreviated version of the classic brand position. However, in each case, there is rationale for the position and a brand personality that may be delivered on a creative brief. These are positioning statements that clarify what a company stands for. That is the essence of positioning.

Changing the Components of Brand Positioning

The brand positioning statement is a very useful strategic tool for testing various ways of looking at your brand's position. This is particularly true when you are looking at how your brand should be positioned with different audiences. Does the brand deliver the same benefit to different groups? For some brands that are based on functional benefits, the answer is likely to be yes. However, when you brand is based on delivering an emotional benefit, the answer may be no.

The following is an example from Victoria's Secret. They have a distinctive brand but they may position the brand slightly differently depending upon what audience they are targeting. Here is one brand positioning statement.

- Victoria's Secret Target One: "To young, single, urban women, Victoria's Secret is the brand of alluring lingerie that will make them feel *secretly sexy.*"

For this young, hip crowd, Victoria's Secret is positioned as a secret confidence builder. The idea is that when you where Victoria's Secret lingerie, you feel different. It makes you more alluring. Now let's see how it is positioned with an older audience.

- Victoria's Secret Target Two: "To married women over fifty, Victoria's Secret is the brand of alluring lingerie that will *reignite the passion in their marriage.*"

For this more mature group, Victoria's Secret is positioned as a marital aid. The idea is that by wearing Victoria's Secret lingerie, you can break out of the same routine. It allows you to be someone a bit new and exciting. While Victoria's Secret has the same overall look and feel, there are subtle positioning differences that it can have depending upon the audience that it is targeting.

The brand positioning statement can be used to vet different positions, different targets, and even different frames of reference.

Competitive Brand Positioning Matrix

This brings us to assessing whether the brand position is unique. Hopefully, you have carved out a position that no one else can occupy. A great positioning should contain these four attributes:

- *Desirable:* The position should be something that the consumer wants. It must fulfill either a functional or emotional need.
- *Distinctive:* The position should be distinctive. No other brand should be able to occupy it. And consumers should perceive it as being unique.
- *Deliverable:* The position needs to be deliverable by the brand. There is no need to position a brand in a certain way if it can't live up to the promise.
- *Durable:* The position needs to be durable. It should be able to last for some time.

One way to assess the brand's position and to make sure it is crystal clear is to develop a brand positioning matrix where you compare your brand to the competition. Figure 10.3 is a brand positioning template that can be used for this task.

This is a great tool with which to play "what if" games with your brand's positioning. For example, you may want to change the target audience or the need state to determine how that action could impact the brand's benefits.

Figure10.3 **Brand Positioning Matrix**

Brand/product	Target definition (demographic usage)	Target market (including need state)	Competitive set	Benefit	Reason why	Brand personality
Your brand						
Competition 1						
Competition 2						
Competition 3						

This is a particularly useful analysis if a competitor has a stronghold on a certain target segment and you want to crack it. In the case of Chef Boyardee, the competition is Franco-American SpaghettiOs. SpaghettiOs were clearly the favorite canned pasta. SpaghettiOs positioned them as being very kidlike and a bit silly. Chef Boyardee countered this by positioning themselves as being for "big kids" and was much more aggressive and masculine. The brand positioning matrix can be a tool to see what dimensions of the positioning you can change and own.

Owning Conceptual Space

The classic brand positioning statement and competitive matrix are staples of the consumer packaged-goods industry. Most brands of consumer packaged goods use some variation of these tools in their marketing process.

Although these classic positioning tools can be readily applied to any category, sometimes they can be a bit of a forced fit. When you are working on categories outside the consumer packaged-goods arena, such as retail, service, or business-to-business marketers, it may be more helpful to look at owning conceptual space.

Conceptual space sounds mystical but it is a fairly simple notion. Conceptual space describes a specific attribute, consumer benefit, or personality trait that is associated specifically with a specific brand. For example, Walmart owns "price" in the consumer's mind. Volvo owns "safety." Rolex owns "luxury."

When you think about owning conceptual space, you start by asking some fundamental questions:

1. What does the consumer want in this category?
2. What are the two key dimensions that are important in the category?
3. What companies are strongly associated with these dimensions?
4. Is there a space in these wants that isn't currently being occupied?
5. Can our brand occupy this space in a credible manner?
6. What personality attributes are most compelling about the category?
7. Does our brand align with the category personality or should it seek another space?

To develop a framework for conceptual space, you can use a simple perceptual mapping technique. This technique uses a horizontal and vertical axis. You plot opposites on each axis. There are a number of ways to do it. The following are four broad areas that can be explored.

- Attribute map: This is mapping the attributes of the category. For example, in the candy category there is chocolate versus nonchocolate and creamy versus chewy.
- Benefit map: This is mapping the category benefits. For example, in the household cleaner category there is gentle versus strong and convenient versus thorough.
- Value map: This is mapping the values of the category. For example, in the wristwatch category there is traditional versus modern and popular versus luxury.
- Personality map: This is mapping personality attributes. For example, in the clothing category there is young versus old and traditional versus trendy.

You can certainly mix and match these areas. You can put the category benefits on one axis and personality on the other axis. The idea is to get the important consumer dimensions for that category and determine if all brands are occupying the same space in the consumers mind.

Let's take a look at the value map for the wristwatch category shown in Figure 10.4. You can see the dimensions of traditional versus modern and popular versus luxury. In this category, there are some very distinct positions that have been created. Rolex occupies the traditional luxury space. Swatch occupies the modern popular space. Tag Heuer has been positioned against Rolex in the luxury space as a more modern alternative. Imports such as Seiko and others fall into the traditional popular space.

In this crowded wristwatch category, you may want to slice it even further to find a position to occupy. For example, you might add a personality dimension to a single quadrant such as traditional luxury. You could evaluate the dimension of sensuous to masculine or sophisticated to trendy. All you are looking for is an area where you can stand out. Owning conceptual space is usually a function of developing your position goal.

What Business Are You In?

Another way to approach the positioning question is to ask, "What business are you in?" This seemingly innocuous question can really make for some interesting discussion. Theodore Leavitt's classic article in the *Harvard Business Review,* "Marketing Myopia," raised the central issue of how you view the business in which you operate. One of the examples he cited in the article was the railroad industry. In the mid-1900s, the railroad industry was the key method of transportation for personal travel as well as freight shipping. However, when other forms of transportation came on the scene

Figure 10.4   **Brand Positioning**

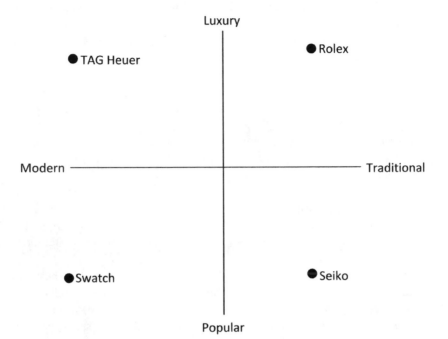

the railroad industry didn't pay any attention since they assumed that they were in the railroad business and not the transportation business.

Another example at that time was the motion picture industry. It once viewed itself in a narrow realm of making movies. However, with the advent of television and so many different content distribution platforms, this industry now views itself as being in the entertainment industry.

The question "What business are you in?" can be used in a similar manner to developing a benefit ladder. In the benefit ladder, you begin with a brand's attributes, move to the brand's functional benefits, and then to the emotional benefits. For example, in the railroad industry, the brand's attributes are the trains and track and people who make it work. The benefit of the industry is that it is a mode of transportation. It gets people and packages to where they need to go. That was the point of Leavitt's article. Businesses should look at themselves for the benefit that they deliver and not the attributes that they have collected.

This exercise works when you look at your industry from a consumer emotional benefit perspective. Let's look at the furniture industry. A furniture retailer isn't just a seller of furniture; they are in the home furnishing business. The benefit is that they help make a house a home. From an emotional perspective, they may well be in the "self-expression" business. Consumers buy furniture just like they buy clothing. It is an expression of their individual tastes. Self-expression is a much broader thought than selling pieces of furniture. It can lead to a series of decisions from merchandising to marketing and ultimately to advertising.

Laws of Positioning

You can't talk about brand positioning without discussing Jack Trout and Al Reis. In their series of books regarding positioning, including *Marketing Warfare, Positioning: The Battle for Your Mind,* and *The 22 Immutable Laws of Marketing,* Trout and Reis brought to light what positioning is and how it can be used to push a company forward. Any student or professional should read these books. They serve as a backbone of literature on this topic.

There are two laws that Trout and Reis cite that are particularly important when you apply them to an advertising campaign. The initial law is that "Being First Is Best." This law states that being the first to do something makes you the most memorable and can lead to owning that position. Even though there have been a number of men who have gone to the moon, the first was Neil Armstrong. He is associated with that event. Miller Lite was the first light beer. It is associated with that even though there are a ton of light beers on the market today. "Subservient Chicken," a viral video from Crispin Porter & Bogusky for Burger King was the first-large scale viral video on YouTube. Thousands of viral videos have since been released but this one stands out as being the first.

The point to the Law of Being First is that developing a memorable positioning and subsequent memorable communication can be greatly enhanced if you are creating "firsts." Whether it is doing something new or creating a new portion of a category, finding that new area will create a differentiated position.

The second law is that most categories come down to two companies or two ideas. There is typically a leading company and then a second-place player followed by a number of niche brands: There is Coke and Pepsi. There is Microsoft and Apple. There is McDonald's and Burger King. Unless you are the leader in the category, you should look to counter the position pegged to the marketplace leader. Southwest Airlines is a great example of going against the grain of all other national and international airlines. Avis took on Hertz. Apple paints all PCs as being the same. The point is that the consumer likes to make things simple. They want decisions to be easy. Categorizing various purchase decisions into groups is one way they do it. As an account planner, you can use this knowledge to develop a position against the category leader where you stand out.

In summary, brand positioning is one of the single most important aspects of managing a brand and developing an award-winning advertising campaign. Much effort should be put into this exercise. Consumer packaged-goods brands have pioneered this concept and are adept at honing a clear and distinctive position. Other marketers are catching up but sometimes have different needs when it comes to the development of a position. As an account planner, you need to adjust your thinking depending upon the product, good, or service with which you are involved. Regardless of how you develop positioning from classic brand positioning statement to finding conceptual space, the proper brand position lays the groundwork for effectively developing an award-winning advertising campaign.

Review Questions

1. How does positioning work? What alternative approaches might be used instead of classic brand positioning?
2. Can positioning be used for services as well as consumer package goods?
3. Can positioning be used for ideas? How? Give examples.
4. Does positioning relate more directly to benefits or to attributes of a brand?

Discussion Questions

1. What is the difference between a positioning strategy and an assault strategy?
2. What is the difference between a positioning and the use of an advertising slogan or "tag line"?
3. How do people position themselves?
4. How do politicians position themselves?
5. How can brand positioning be transferred into a personality matrix?

Additional Resources

Mark, M., and C. Pearson, C. *The Hero and the Outlaw: Building Extraordinary Brands through the Power of Archetypes.* Maidenhead, Berkshire, England: McGraw-Hill, 2001.

Ries, A., and J. Trout. *Positioning: The Battle for Your Mind.* New York: McGraw-Hill, 2000.

Chapter 11

Brand Personality

One of the most powerful traits of any brand, company, or person is personality. Just like a person, every company displays some sort of personality traits. A brand can be playful, sophisticated, down home, or even sexy. Some brands have a personality by default. Other brands nurture their personality just like they do the features that go into the brand. They understand that personality can play a huge role in distinguishing one brand from another.

As an account planner, your role is to help the brand recognize the importance of cultivating its personality. It can be a very powerful marketing tool both inside and outside the company. Defining the brand's personality is also a crucial aspect of developing an award-winning campaign. Before advertising is conceived, the creative team must understand the brand's personality. It is similar to an actor understanding his character's traits. It is crucial to the makeup of the character in a play and it is equally as important to the makeup of a brand.

Why Brand Personality Is Important

Many executives may think that their role is to find tangible ways to make their brand different from their competitors. They spend countless hours and dollars to discover their brand's "point of difference." Often this is expressed through the human qualities that can be ascribed to the brand. A brand's personality is its human characteristics. If you were describing the brand as a person, what adjectives would you use to describe it?

While a brand personality may seem like a "touchy-feely" thing that may have no business merit, it is far from that. A well-nurtured brand personality can be a key distinguishing factor that separates one brand from another. Just as much effort needs to be put into staying true to the brand's character or personality as driving home the brand's benefit.

The brand personality can be more enduring than a functional benefit. It can be as strong as zeroing in on an emotional benefit. This is particularly true in categories where it is difficult to gain a compelling edge or unique feature. Let's face it, is there really any difference between one bank and another? Or is there anything unique about a gas station or do you just go to the one that is more convenient? From a functional benefit perspective, all banks and gas stations are pretty much alike. Where a brand can stand out is in the area of brand personality.

Competitors in the insurance category provide a classic example of personality differences between brands. Most insurance companies are working to be sincere, trustworthy, and down-to-earth. "Like a Good Neighbor, State Farm is there," "You are in good hands with Allstate," and "Nationwide is on your side" are all examples of brands with similar personalities. Then Geico entered the scene and went with a totally different personality. It was brash, irreverent, and fun. With its myriad of characters from the gecko to the cavemen, Geico carved out a niche in the market with its brand personality to go along with the compelling benefit, "15 minutes can save you 15 percent."

Some categories that are built with brand personality as the lead ingredient. All fashion categories, such as clothing, perfume, and cosmetics are very much influenced by personality. Leisure products such as golf and tennis apparel and equipment take on the personality of the athletes that endorse them. There is a big difference between Phil Mickelson and Tiger Woods. Each of these celebrity athletes evokes a certain personality.

Nike has built its business on personality-driven athletic performance equipment. Motorcycles, fishing gear, and even sports franchises have big personality components as their main points of difference. Carving out a unique brand personality can have a huge financial benefit. It is many times stronger and more enduring than the functional benefit, which may have introduced the brand. Personality should be treated with the same respect as the other aspects of brand positioning.

Brand Personality and Advertising Tone

Many people confuse brand personality with the tone of the advertising. Many advertising executives have had their clients ask them to create a personality for their brand through advertising. Advertising can be a key ingredient to magnifying and expanding or sometimes changing a brand's personality. But it is not the only aspect of the personality mix.

The sentiment expressed in the old saying, "You can put a dress on a pig but it's still a pig," can present a challenge when dealing with brand personality. For example, if the consumer experience in a retail setting is that the employees are rude and don't care, no amount of advertising "hype" will likely persuade them that shopping in that store is really fun and exciting. The company would have to make a real effort to change its ways before the advertising could be effective.

Brand personality is the total package. This is particularly true in service companies and retailers who literally touch consumers. When there is face-to-face contact with the customer, the brand personality is up close and very personal.

Defining a Brand's Personality

There are a number of schemes for defining brand personality. Research companies and advertising agencies have their own proprietary methods for defining and profiling a brand's personality. One of the classic published works on the topic is David Aaker's book, *Building Strong Brands,* in which he outlines a brand personality scale categorizing brands into the "Big 5 Personalities." The five groups are: sincerity, excitement, competence, sophistication, and ruggedness.

Aaker found that in extensive research with 1,000 respondents who rated 60 brands using 114 different personality traits, the Big 5 explained 93 percent of all observed differences between these brands. This either says it is a great study or that most brands are pretty similar. The truth is that this method of categorization is effective and should be considered a necessary tool for any account planner.

Figure 11.1 shows the Big 5 Personality groups. You will notice that there are subgroups and subgroups to the subgroups. For example, under the sincerity umbrella are the down-to-earth, honest, wholesome, and cheerful subgroups. These are directions a brand in the sincerity arena can migrate toward. The cheerful subgroup is further refined to include sentimental, friendly, warm, and happy. The point of this subgrouping is to cover and categorize each personality trait.

This is important either to gain some distance from another brand or to reposition your brand in a more favorable light. Walmart is certainly in the sincerity category and falls into the down-to-earth subgroup. You could make the case that Walmart has a very small-town personality and feel. As they have grown, they have likely moved away from their small-town feel to more generally family oriented. They are still down-to-earth but the subtle personality traits of the brand have likely changed over time.

As you assess a brand, remember that, just like a person, no one brand fits neatly into any or all of these five categories. You are likely to have a dominant trait and a less dominant personality trait. For example, a brand like McDonald's is in the sincerity category. Ronald McDonald is all about sincerity. However, the McDonald's company and brand also has an air of competence. They are an extremely efficient operation, from how they prepare the food to how they keep their restaurants clean. BMW would be in both the excitement and sophistication categories.

Figure 11.1 **Brand Personality Scale**

A Brand Personality Scale (BPS): The Big 5

Sincerity (Campbell's, Hallmark, Kodak)
- Down-to-Earth: family-oriented, small-town, conventional, blue-collar, all-American
- Honest: sincere, real, ethical, thoughtful, caring
- Wholesome: original, genuine, ageless, classic, old-fashioned
- Cheerful: sentimental, friendly, warm, happy

Excitement (Porsche, Absolute, Benetton)
- Daring: trendy, exciting, off-beat, flashy, provocative
- Spirited: cool, young, lively, outgoing, adventurous
- Imaginative: unique, humorous, surprising, artistic, fun
- Up-to-date: independent, contemporary, innovative, aggressive

Competence (AMEX, CNN, IBM)
- Reliable: hardworking, secure, efficient, trustworthy, careful
- Intelligent: technical, corporate, serious
- Successful: leader, confident, influential

Sophistication (Lexus, Mercedes, Revlon)
- Upper class: glamorous, good-looking, pretentious, sophisticated
- Charming: feminine, smooth, sexy, gentle

Ruggedness (Levi's, Marlboro, Nike)
- Outdoorsy: masculine, western, active, athletic
- Tough: rugged, strong, no-nonsense

Source: Reprinted with the permission of The Free Press, a Division of Simon & Schuster Adult Publishing Group, from *Building Strong Brands* by David Aaker. Copyright © 1996 by David A. Aaker. All rights reserved.

You can use the brand personality scale to measure the degree to which the personality categories and traits reflect the brand. You can also compare one brand to another to see where you might be able to exploit some differences. Sometimes it is as important to understand what your brand isn't as much as what it is.

Figure 11.2 illustrates how you can relate a seven-point scale to each of the brand personality categories. The example reflects McDonald's, which has a good sincerity association but not sophistication or ruggedness. As you direct advertising executions, you wouldn't want to see Ronald McDonald dressed like James Bond or getting into a knife fight. This would be a bit out of character for the brand. The biggest area of opportunity for the brand is to dial up its excitement level. While McDonald's may not be exciting to teens or adults, it certainly is exciting to young children. There is a component of family excitement for the brand.

Figure 11.2   **Big 5 Personality Linkage**

Big Five Personality Linkage						
McDonald's						
Doesn't Explain						Explains Very Well
Sincerity	○	○	○	○	○	○	●
Excitement	○	○	●	○	○	○	○
Sophistication	●	○	○	○	○	○	○
Competence	○	○	○	○	●	○	○
Ruggedness	●	○	○	○	○	○	○

Challenging the Category Personality

Most people have a feeling about goods and services that are available in the marketplace. For example, you may think jewelry is sophisticated or exciting, you likely would want your electricity provider to be reliable, and you probably feel your stockbroker should be savvy and serious about your money.

Every product category has a personality profile. It is part of what you expect to gain or experience when you are purchasing this good or service. For the most part, the category leader takes on the overall personality of the category. In Figure 11.3, we have listed four categories and the category leader in each. While their brand personalities are different, they do follow a pattern. Most people expect their banks to be pretty serious. After all, it is your money. You don't want some silly person handling your money, do you? Yet, in our example for Bank United they used this understanding to their advantage and went against the banking stereotype.

In fact, as you eye each of these categories, you may see another pattern emerge. Going against the expected personality of a category may yield very good results. Apple Computers is the anti-IBM. While IBM is very corporate, Apple doesn't take itself too seriously. Apple went against the category and the leader to carve out an interesting business and personality niche.

In the cosmetics arena, the majority of brands possess some level of sophistication. Some brands are more contemporary than others, Estée Lauder having an older clientele versus Clinique with a more youthful customer group, but for the most part, cosmetics play to women's aspirational desires. Ironically, Mary Kay Cosmetics built a business by going against the grain in nearly every aspect of the category. Mary Kay is sold in the home by a neighbor, their packages are plain and they sell natural products. They are about as down-home as you can get in a category that can be very pretentious.

Figure 11.3

Personality				
		Category Positioning Exercise		
Category	**Expected Personality**	**Category Leader**	**Personality**	**Opposite Personality**
Cosmetics	Sophistication	Clinique	Sophistication	Down-home
Computers	Corporate	IBM	Corporate	Fun
Motorcycles	Rugged	Harley Davidson	Rugged	Gentle
Banking	Serious	Bank of America	Serious	Silly

Even in the motorcycle area there are contrasts to some of the major brands. You expect a motorcycle to be pretty rugged. Harley-Davidson has capitalized on this fact by having more white-collar "weekend warriors" riding their motorcycles than members of Hells Angels. Contrast this with Honda who presents a gentler image of getting back to nature by riding a motorcycle.

Personality can be a real differentiator and it can be used strategically to attack a category, not only from an advertising or brand perspective, but from a business perspective as well.

How to Define Brand Personality

There are a lot of research techniques for helping define a brand personality. One of the typical methods used to help sort out one brand's personality from another is through a word association test.

In a word association test, a respondent is asked to assign words that best fit the brand. This can be done by free association, where a respondent rattles off words that first come to mind to describe a brand, or through a written exercise, where the researcher gives the respondent words to associate with the brand.

Figure 11.4 is an example of a portion of a word association test where respondents were asked to use a semantic differential scale to associate brands. In this case, you ask the respondent to classify a brand from one extreme to another to assess the association. The example before you shows the differences between Budweiser beer and Corona beer. You can see the two beers have very different associations. Budweiser is heavily associated with being masculine, blue collar, old-fashioned, real, and plain. On the other hand, Corona is a bit more feminine, contemporary, and sexy. Both brands lie somewhere between humorous and serious.

Depending upon the brand and the intent of the exercise, you can add as many pairs of descriptors as you feel is necessary to get a read on the brand's personality association.

Figure 11.4 **Two Brand Comparison**

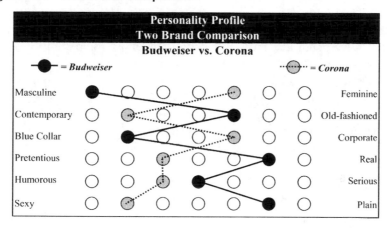

There are other qualitative techniques commonly used to round out a brand's personality profile. One such technique is a picture sort where consumers look at a variety of pictures and pick the ones that best fit the brand. Many researchers use a range of drinks, cars, shoes, or houses to determine the associations. Other researchers ask consumers to bring in pictures they feel represent the brand. From there, the researcher will ask probing questions to get at the emotions the consumer might associate with the brand.

Other associations that are popular are famous people or celebrities. You can ask a consumer, if this brand were a celebrity who would it be? Any range of items that can demonstrate a personality or emotional range is fair game. It is important to be consistent and to use the same technique for each product or service brand to gain some sort of validation and base of experience. These projection techniques allow consumers to stretch their minds when discussing your brand.

One last method is a sensory technique in which the consumer is asked to discuss a brand using each of the senses. For example, you could ask the consumer to listen to various musical excerpts and ask which of them describes the brand. You could provide scent samples and ask which of them relates to the brand. Sensory reactions can help draw out a brand story or personality.

Developing a Brand Story

The majority of marketing and advertising research is very much on the informational side of the ledger. This is why developing the brand personality is so important. It helps to humanize the brand. Knowing the brand personality is one step toward understanding how to best link the brand's values to the values humans desire. An emotional connection creates a much stronger bond than functional benefit alone.

Personality, in and of itself, is not the stopping point for creative exploration. Advertising that provides drama is the most compelling. Just like *Hamlet,* a brand is made up of story ingredients. A story typically includes a lead character, a setting, other characters, a source of conflict or opposition, symbolism, mood, and a plot (Figure 11.5).

Like a novelist creating a story, an account planner looks for the drama inherent to the product. An account planner or a qualitative researcher probes the following areas to ascertain story elements that describe a brand:

1. Setting: Where is the product most enjoyed?
2. Characters: What role does it play in relationships between people?
3. Opposition: What are the relevant conflicts or oppositions?
4. Symbols: What aspects of people's experience of the product suggest symbols or metaphors?
5. Mood: How do people feel when using the product?
6. Plot: What role does the product play in a sequence of events?

In each of these areas comprising a story, we are looking for memory cues or what novelist Cecilia Bartholomew calls "irrelevancies." These are seemingly unimportant pieces of information that give daily life emotional texture. For example, sitting in your pajamas while sipping coffee and reading the morning paper is a string of irrelevancies. However, if you were advertising Folgers brand coffee, those irrelevancies might make for a compelling coffee story or bring the brand's personality to life. Let's face it, Jerry Seinfeld has made a great comedic career out of bringing irrelevancies to life. It is the account planners' job to investigate brands at this level to determine if there are social links that can be exploited by the brand.

There are a number of ways to get after the brand's story. One method is to ask consumers to write their own brand story. By allowing consumers to write a story you can get a much deeper sense of the brand's personality and linkage to real life events. When you have ten individual stories, you can then edit them into a single story for the brand.

The more traditional way to get at the brand's story is through ethnographic research in which a researcher spends time with the brand user or family when they are using the product. For example, the researcher might go home with mom and observe her preparing the family meal and the family enjoying it. After observing a number of consumer respondents, the ethnographic researcher analyzes his observations and the brand story they imply.

Figure 11.6 illustrates an example of a brand story for Kool-Aid from

Figure 11.5   **Plotting Circle**

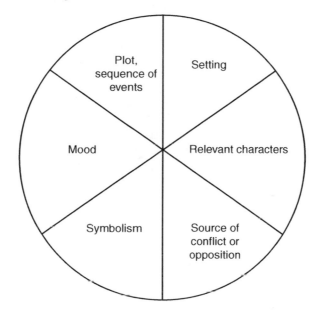

an article by Jeffrey Durgee, "Understanding Brand Personality." Through qualitative research techniques, consumers were asked to fill in the story line for the Kool-Aid brand.

As you can see from this example, a lot of symbolism and many metaphors are used when discussing this brand. The pitcher itself has become an icon for the brand. The pitcher magically turning colors is a transforming experience. The brand is also very active with reference to standing or hiking while drinking. It is also a social drink enjoyed at home and elsewhere.

The storytelling technique adds tremendous texture to the brand personality. It is a critical aspect of taking the brand personality to the next level. As an account planner, you will want to use both traditional research such as word association and other tests to draw out the brand's personality. Then you should add texture to the outline of this personality profile through storytelling explorations.

Brand personality is an important ingredient for any brand or company. It can be a powerful competitive advantage and it is one of the key elements for creating compelling advertising.

Review Questions

    1. Why is it important for a brand to have a personality?
    2. How does brand personality relate to product positioning?

Figure 11.6   **Kool Aid Basic Wants**

Source: J. Durgee, "Understanding Brand Personality," *Journal of Consumer Marketing* 5(3) pp. 21–25: 1988.

3. How are brand positioning and category positioning similar? How are they different?

Discussion Questions

1. How can a brand's personality be linked to its advertising and other promotions?
2. Why does a brand need a story with a plot? How can advertising contribute to this story?
3. What brands can you think of that have stories included in their advertising?

Additional Resources

Aaker, D. *Building Strong Brands.* New York: Free Press, 1996.

Harrison, S. *IdeaSpotting: How to Find Your Next Great Idea.* Georgetown, Ontario, Canada: Fraser Direct, 2006.

Harrison, S. *Zing! Five Steps and 101 Tips for Creativity on Command.* Canada: Machillock, 2004.

Chapter 12

Brand Essence

Defining a brand's essence is like defining a great story or a movie. They both have a number of layers. They each start with an idea. They work to connect at an emotional level with their audience. To develop an award-winning advertising campaign, one of the key aspects is to identify the brand's essence. A brand's essence is one or two words that capture what the brand is all about. It sums up the brand's position, its benefits, its personality, and its character in a simple statement.

Brands start as either a product or a company. The Apple computer was developed as an alternative to Microsoft's PC. Rather than opening up their operating system to a host of manufacturers like Microsoft did with Windows, the Apple system is only available on a Mac. Now, that fact is one attribute of the Apple computer. That is one aspect of the brand. The benefits of Apple are that it is simple, it is vulnerable to fewer viruses than an open system, and it has more design features. But, there is a host of other things that make up the Apple brand. Its unique name, logo, slogan, and design are all parts of it. Its iconic advertising is another. The almost obsessive loyalty among its user base is another. Its essence is "unleashing creativity." Those few words describe everything about the brand. You are looking for a brief symbolic embodiment of all the information and inspiration connected to the company or product or service.

Most companies or products are developed to fill a consumer need. They start off based on some observation about a business category or an unmet consumer need. State Farm Insurance, the number one insurance company in the United States, started this way. In 1922, George Jacob Mecherle, a farmer and insurance agent, suggested to his boss that farmers should pay less for auto insurance since they drove fewer miles and had fewer accidents than city folks. His boss disagreed and suggested to Mr. Mecherle that if that's what he wanted to do, then he should start his own insurance business. So he did. The simple concept of rate fairness set into motion what is now one of the largest independent companies in the country.

The point is that brands start with an idea that changes the way you think about a product category or helps create a new category. Over time, these business ideas take on human qualities. People can relate to them. Certain brands and businesses evoke strong feelings and attachments. Some products are worn like a badge. They help describe the person. Many times what a brand becomes from an emotional perspective outweighs what it actually delivers as a basic product. Why are there hundreds of brands of bottled water? The majority come from the same place, the municipal water system. Yet we form feelings and relationships with different brands.

To create an award-winning campaign, it is crucial to understand every aspect of the brand you are marketing. The goal is to get to the core of the brand or its essence, starting with a fundamental understanding of why the brand was developed in the first place and ending with how it fits into a consumer's life. Getting at a brand's essence is a culmination of all the brand positioning work and countless hours of planning and research you will do to ensure that your brand stands out from the rest.

Understand the Attribute

The brand essence begins with the brand's attributes. All products, services, retailers and companies have unique attributes that make up their business. If they did not have something of substance, they would have no reason to exist. Attributes are used to compare brands or businesses. This is why businesses are driven to produce unique attributes. They are constantly trying to differentiate themselves from their competitors. Product attributes for packaged-good products are typically called features. Other businesses such as retailers, service businesses, and business-to-business marketers typically have attributes that are born out of unique business practices. While a packaged-good product might have a unique selling proposition, a retailer, service, or business-to-business marketer may have a unique business proposition.

Table 12.1 lists common attributes for different categories of business. Let's take a look at products. Discovering product attributes is one of the easiest and most common factors in buyer behavior in our life. For example, a floor cleaner manufacturer may add lemon to mask the ammonia smell of their cleaning liquid. The lemon smell is a product feature. Most mustard brands now come in a squeeze bottle that makes them easier to use. M&M's come in various sizes and colors and can contain nuts and different types of chocolate. Again, these are all product features. You can go down the list of common product attributes and think of everyday products that have unique tastes, sounds, shapes, and smells.

Table 12.1

Common Attributes

Products	Retail
Substance	Store design
Structure	Hours open
Color	Merchandise
Shape	Delivery
Texture	Sales personnel
Sound	Pricing (EDLP vs. sales)
Taste	Logistics
Odor	
Packaging	
Ingredients	
Patent	

B2B	Service
Patent	Customer service
Customer service	Geographic coverage
Distribution	Price
Unique process or method	Distribution/delivery
Price	Unique process/method
Area of expertise	
Geographic coverage	

Now let's take a look at retailing. Most retailers define themselves by the merchandise they carry. Some are in business based on delivering just merchandise such as The Gap clothing story. The Gap is all about delivering the basic look. Their stores reflect the simplicity of their merchandise. As you look at these standard retail attributes, you have surely seen them in action. Do you remember the first 24-hour grocery store? The 7/11 convenience store brand was named after the hours it kept. Other concepts such as the dollar stores have taken the price attribute as their claim to fame. The number one furniture retailer in the country built his business on same-day delivery. While other furniture stores made you wait months for your order, Gallery Furniture in Houston, Texas, developed a method for same-day delivery. This unique approach to business now helps them generate over $100 million in sales from a single location. Now *that* is one powerful attribute.

Many service-based companies began as a result of developing a unique attribute or business method. Federal Express used a central hub system to deliver packages overnight. Until Federal Express launched their service, American Airlines and other carriers dominated the package delivery market. They never recovered from Federal Express's business changes. Motel 6 defined their business on a $6-a-night room rate. The price has now crept up past $30 a night, but Motel 6 is still known as an inexpensive motel.

Northern Trust specializes in providing financial support to individuals with high net worth. They have built a model that offers a suite of services for extremely wealthy individuals, ranging from traditional banking to more esoteric services such as philanthropy and complex trusts. Northern Trust is carving out a point of difference in the field of financial institutions. Services with a unique business proposition or method are the ones that are most successful.

One area that doesn't get the press of the above categories is business-to-business marketing. Yet businesses are developed every day on unique attributes or business propositions. One such business is Administaff, which provides employee benefits for small businesses. Administaff is unique because they put employees on their payroll. By consolidating numerous small businesses in this way, Administaff is able to get better prices on health insurance and other employee benefits than a small business could on its own. Matlock Tools sells tools only to construction workers. They drive a tool van to job sites and sell their tools right out of the van. Cisco Systems provides the routers that help move information from one computer or server to another. Their special patents make them a leader in this rapidly changing technology field.

A strong business can be built on a unique attribute or business method. As an account planner, it is your job to help businesses make the leap from a business attribute to a consumer benefit.

Attribute Versus Benefit

Consumers react positively to goods and services that provide benefits. The benefit is the customer's reward for using the product. While you can build a successful business based on a unique attribute or business model, a strong brand or piece of communication requires a strong benefit.

Just to reiterate, what a product, service or business does for the consumer is called a benefit. In many marketing textbooks, it is also called a functional benefit. It is called a functional benefit because it describes what the brand does or how it functions or performs to benefit the customer. Most marketers just call it a benefit unless they are referencing an emotional benefit, which we will talk about a little later.

For now, let's discuss the functional benefit. The functional benefit is probably the most frequently used benefit type in brand positioning and in advertising copy. When you have the first of a kind or new product "news," then the functional benefit may be the best thing to promote. For example, if you are the first hybrid car to run on gas and electricity, you may want to promote the functional benefit of getting 75 miles to a gallon of gas. In

Table 12.2

Attribute to Functional Benefit

Consumer Product: Hunt's Tomato

Attributes	Functional benefit
100% ACV	Find it in any store
Made with vine-ripened tomatoes	Fresh-tasting tomatoes
Contains lycopene	Natural source of antioxidants
Over 20 varieties	Fits whatever you are cooking

Retailer: Home Depot

Attributes	Functional benefit
Low-price guarantee	Always get best price
Hire former tradesmen as personnel	Expert advice
Carry name-brand merchandise	Find the brands I am familiar with
Deliver to job site	Convenient, saves time

Service: Southwest Airlines

Attributes	Functional benefit
Fleet of planes all same model, which makes for easy service	Reliable service
Fly to close-in city airports	Convenient business travel
Low everyday fares	Inexpensive travel
Encourage flight attendants to have fun	Pleasant experience

Business-to-Business: Waste Management

Attributes	Functional benefit
Only national company for hauling and landfills	Take care of my needs no matter how large my company becomes
All landfills are EPA certified	My waste will be in compliance with government regulations
Largest recycler in the United States	Establish and execute my recycling program
Use landfills to make methane gas to fuel their fleets	Environmentally conscious and innovative

today's environment, where gas costs around $3.00 a gallon, this is a pretty compelling message. If McDonald's introduces a 19-cent hamburger, it doesn't take a genius to figure out it's a good deal. The functional benefit is that you can eat a complete meal for under a buck. Now that sounds good when you are pinching pennies.

In Table 12.2 we have listed a series of products, goods, and services that have unique attributes with their corresponding functional benefits. Let's walk through the examples to see how the categories differ in terms of turning a business attribute into a consumer benefit.

In the example, we have selected Hunt's tomato products. Hunt's is the leader in canned tomato products. As you can see, they have some solid attributes. They have 100 percent all commodity volume (ACV), which is an industry term for grocery distribution. In Hunt's case, their products are in all of the grocery stores so the benefit is that no matter where you shop at you will find their products. Hunt's also has a taste benefit. They select only vine-ripened tomatoes, which are the best tasting. Hunt's has a health benefit as well. Tomatoes contain lycopene, a natural source of antioxidants, which helps prevent certain forms of cancer. One other benefit Hunt's brings to consumers is they have over twenty varieties of products. The benefit is you can find a Hunt's product to suit a number of recipes.

As an account planner, there are number of ways to communicate the benefits of Hunt's. You could focus on the taste of the vine-ripened tomatoes or you may direct your efforts to capitalize on the growing senior citizen population with a health message. Perhaps you would be wise to communicate the variety of dishes that are easy to make with Hunt's products. Depending upon your objective, you may favor one approach over another.

Let's take a look at our retail example with the leading home improvement retailer, Home Depot. Home Depot has a number of great business attributes that have made them very successful. They have put into place a low-price guarantee meaning they will match any price on the same item if you see it advertised lower somewhere else. Walmart has used the low-price attribute as their "killer attribute" for years. As a result most other big box retailers use a low-price guarantee to combat Walmart and other discount operations. Home Depot has also distinguished itself from the competition by hiring former tradesman as sales personnel. For the average homeowner, this is a huge benefit when you have a project to do. Finding someone who can give you the proper advice and all the right materials to get the job done right is a strong consumer benefit. For the commercial trades, Home Depot has a separate check-out area and will deliver materials to a job site. They are making it as convenient as possible for the contractor, saving them time and money.

It may come as no big surprise that Home Depot has for years run advertising that reflects their people helping homeowners solve problems. While Home Depot advertises certain merchandise at selective price points, their umbrella advertising campaign of "You can do it. We can help" emphasizes the function benefit.

Service organizations such as Southwest Airlines have characteristics similar to those of retailers. Both make an investment in their employees through good salaries, reward systems and opportunities for advancement. This is important because their staff delivers the product. Southwest Airlines has revolutionized airline travel with some unusual business practices. Unlike other airlines, Southwest flies only one type of aircraft. This has become a huge competitive advantage for them. It makes the maintenance easier, holds down costs, and increases reliability. They also keep costs down by focusing on shorter trips, no food on the flight, and no first class, which would mean additional attendants. The result is lower fares. Southwest also encourages their flight attendants to be irreverent. While the lack of extras could be a point of annoyance for business travelers, it is actually kind of fun to fly on Southwest Airlines. This is also what they choose to advertise to counterbalance the "no frills" aspect of the actual experience.

As you can see from the examples, packaged goods are very easy to move from attribute to benefit. Retail and service companies are a bit more challenging since their business attributes don't always make for compelling advertising benefits. The challenge is to balance what may be more compelling copy with what is the greatest attribute. The most challenging area to derive customer benefits from business attributes is in the business-to-business area.

Let's take a look at our example of Waste Management. Picking up trash and moving it to a landfill isn't exactly the most glamorous job, but it certainly is a necessity of life. While Waste Management does pick up residential trash, their main revenue generators are commercial trash collection and landfill management. They are also the largest recycling company in North America. Imagine for a moment you are the head of Ford Motor Company's plants. You have some pretty nasty and toxic waste to dispose of and, because you are a publicly traded company, you have significant shareholder responsibility for ensuring that this is done properly. You would likely be very happy to find a company that was in compliance with government regulations. You might also be able to show you were progressive by recycling certain materials and you could guarantee all the waste was dealt with in a similar manner regardless of the plant location in North America. While waste disposal may not be "top of mind," for some businesspeople it is a huge issue and a potential liability. While compliance may be the most compelling benefit for a large corporation, from a communication perspective you may choose to feature innovation. Most large companies want to associate with other innovative large companies. Rather than scare potential customers with a compliance message, you may want to communicate how innovative you are and by association, how innovative they are.

To define functional benefits, business attributes are viewed from a consumer standpoint. It is what the attribute does for the customer that makes the difference. One of the difficult tasks of the account planner is to ferret out compelling benefits that can be communicated effectively. The greatest business attribute may or may not provide the most compelling message. Many brands have been created by relentlessly advertising their functional benefits. However, there comes a time for many brands when promoting a functional benefit may not be a real point of difference. In this case, you need to look further than a functional benefit to differentiate the brand. You need to look to the emotional benefit.

Emotional Benefits

A great copy book from the pre-television age that sums up emotional versus functional benefits in very commonsense terms. In his 1936 book *How to Write Advertising,* author Kenneth Goode talked about "selling the effect" copy. His example at that period was Simmons mattresses. Simmons was the leader in mattress sales and touted their very comfortable mattress. However, instead of selling a product benefit such as a comfortable mattress, Goode suggested that as the category leader Simmons should consider selling the effect of a good night's sleep instead.

In this case, Goode outlines the "sell the effect-of-the-effect" copy. In the Simmons example, he went on to say that instead of selling the mattress or even "better sleep," Simmons could go even further. A good night's sleep could lead to better health or even personal success. The "effects of the effect" is another way to think about an emotional benefit.

If a functional benefit is a product performance benefit, then the emotional benefit is the personal performance benefit. It is what the product does for an individual's life. Another great example of this is razor blades. Over the years, razor blades have gotten more sophisticated. The product is designed to give a close shave. So, what does having a close shave mean to a man? It might mean the difference between looking their best, which could be the difference between getting a great job or getting the good-looking girl. Who thought a simple razor blade could evoke such emotions? As an account planner, it is your job to help the client and the creative teams see the "effect of the effect." It is important to understand how a brand, service, or company fits into the consumer's life.

Plus or Minus Emotions

One way to think about emotional benefits is that the brand can have one of two effects on a person's life. It can add a positive or it can remove a negative. Does the product add a positive to the consumer's life or keep them from a negative experience?

In the razor blade example, the product can add to someone's life with by making them look better. By looking better, they feel better about themselves, which gives them more confidence. If they are confident about themselves,

Table 12.3

Emotional Benefit

Add a positive experience	Remove a negative experience

Through sensory pleasures:
  Smell
  Taste
  Sight
  Sound
  Tactile
	Removal of negative sensory experience:
	  Body odor
	  Loud noises
	  Sweaty hands

Elevating personal importance:
  Pride
  Recognition
  Gratitude
	Relief from negative aspects of the person:
	  Ridiculed
	  Loathed
	  Disgusting

Through excitement, amusement, or ecstasy	Through removal of fear, sadness, anger, or surprise

they are more likely to get a better job or the girl of their dreams. You get the idea.

Table 12.3 illustrates some of the emotions related to positive and negative experiences. As you look at this list, you can think of products that capitalize on one side of the equation or the other. For example, all deodorants certainly remove a negative. Having body odor is pretty disgusting. So, while the functional benefit of a deodorant is to mask the body's odor, the emotional benefit is to make sure that no one turns up their nose when they get close to you.

As you look at the list of positives and negatives, the one area that is a classic for advertising is the area of sensory pleasures. This can be removing a negative sensory experience such as body odor or adding a sensory experience such as making your clothes smell fresh after they are washed. The senses are a good place to start in terms of identifying emotions that can be released. Consumers want to experience positives whether in taste, sound, sight, or tactile feelings. This is why advertising professionals spend countless hours crafting ads incorporating these sensory elements into the presentation.

In carrying forward our previous examples of Hunt's, Home Depot, Southwest Airlines, and Waste Management, let's see what emotional benefits they might provide. In the case of Hunt's, sensory emotions are obvious. This is why most food advertising has what is called a "bite and smile" aspect to creative execution. You want to show the emotional benefit of people enjoying the great taste of your food. Digging a bit deeper than just the sensory

Table 12.4

Functional Benefits to Emotional Benefits

Brand	Functional benefit	Emotional benefit
Hunt's	Vine-ripened, freshest-tasting tomatoes	Smell and taste of a great meal
		Feel good about serving the best to your family
Home Depot	Expert advice of former tradesmen	Pride in doing your own improvement project
Southwest Airlines	Reliable, inexpensive travel	Freedom to travel whenever you want
Waste Management	All waste will be in government compliance	No surprises in taking care of my needs

emotions, you could make the case that mom is gratified by serving a meal her family loves. This makes her feel pretty good about herself. So, you may be adding some self-esteem to the self-image.

In the case of Home Depot, the consumer feels pride in a job well done. It is an empowering feeling to knock out a home improvement project that might have called for hiring a professional to accomplish. Home Depot's expert sales people gave the consumer more than just the materials and instruction to accomplish the task. They gave him some personal power. Now think about the theme line of their advertising campaign, "You can do it. We can help." It encourages the consumer to feel pride in getting the job done.

Southwest Airlines is a reliable, inexpensive airline. On an emotional level, this is a freeing experience. It gives you the freedom to travel. By removing the barriers of cost, time, and delays, there is an emotional benefit of being able to control your own destiny in travel. It is a release of the travel burden. Southwest Airlines advertising, "You are now free to move about the country," taps into this emotional benefit.

For Waste Management, the functional benefit of ensuring all waste is dealt with in a responsible manner means there will be no surprises. This can be a huge relief for business owners. Waste Management advertising points to this emotional benefit in their slogan, "From everyday collection to environmental protection. Think Green. Think Waste Management." They are selling the idea that they are the good stewards of a business that removes a huge potential negative to the customer's business life.

Emotional benefits are also called higher order benefits (see Table 12.4).

One reason advertisers focus on emotional benefits is that the functional benefits of the product may not be unique or compelling. If every razor blade gives a smooth clean shave, then you need to move to a higher order benefit to help differentiate your brand. In a world of parity products, it is typical for the brand that gets to the emotional benefit first to win in the marketplace. In our examples, the category leaders had some expression of an emotional benefit in their advertising.

If you can capture the emotional benefit of the brand and reflect it compellingly in the advertising, then you have a powerful tool. Consumers may try your brand based on a product feature or functional benefit. However, consumers will bond with you and be much less likely to switch brands if they can connect with you on an emotional level.

Benefit Laddering

Now it is time to put it all together. You understand your product's attributes and how it benefits the consumer both functionally and emotionally. You have a firm grasp on your target market and what makes them tick. One way to pull all this information together is through an exercise called benefit laddering.

Figure 12.1 details a benefit ladder for Tide laundry detergent.

As you can see, the base of the ladder is a description of the target market. In this case it is a mom with a family that has a penchant for getting their clothes dirty. The product, Tide, has some unique attributes that make it a great product. It has special formulas that get clothes clean and leaves them without soap residue, which can break down cloth fiber. The benefit is that Tide gets clothes clean and makes them last longer than other detergents. So how does this help mom? It taps into her cost-conscious head. She feels smart because she doesn't have to buy clothes as often since they stay looking new longer. In this case, Tide may help mom be a hero in a household where the budget is tight.

You can and should do this exercise for any company you are working with. There can be more than one functional and emotional benefit, so just experiment. The foundation of the exercise is the target market. In this case, the Tide consumer was very cost conscious so that is a driving force in solving her problem. Once you have the consumer, then you fill in the product attributes. From there you derive the functional benefit and ladder up into the emotional benefit.

The benefit laddering exercise is a good one to do with company management to get them to continue to explore the higher order benefits of the product or service they are marketing. It is also a common exercise that is

Figure 12.1   **Benefit Ladder: Tide Example**

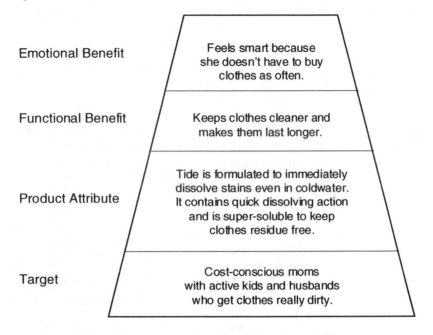

Emotional Benefit	Feels smart because she doesn't have to buy clothes as often.
Functional Benefit	Keeps clothes cleaner and makes them last longer.
Product Attribute	Tide is formulated to immediately dissolve stains even in coldwater. It contains quick dissolving action and is super-soluble to keep clothes residue free.
Target	Cost-conscious moms with active kids and husbands who get clothes really dirty.

done in qualitative research. Researchers will ask consumers either in focus groups or one-on-one settings to describe why they buy a product and then to ladder up into increasingly emotional benefits. For example, the majority of moms are going to say they buy Tide because it gets their clothes clean and makes them last longer. Most people will give a rational answer to the question. However, a good qualitative researcher can begin to ask questions such as, "So, how does that help you?" "How does that make you feel?" or "Does your husband notice it?" With a deeper line of questioning, researchers can help unlock some of the emotional benefits of most products.

Benefit Matrix

Now we are going to throw you a curveball. We have spent this chapter working on how you move from a product attribute to a consumer benefit to an emotional benefit. This is logical, but the problem is that nearly all products, goods, and services have multiple benefits. What makes your task more difficult is that different target markets can have totally different motivations for buying the same product. For example, a Honda Civic is a great first car. Young drivers who are attracted to it find it sporty, easy to handle and accepted by their peers as being cool. Parents, who may be pay-

Table 12.5

Benefit Matrix: Orville Redenbacher Gourmet Popcorn

Target market	Health-conscious moms with 'tweens and teenage kids	Fun-loving 'tweens and girls
Product attribute	Orville Redenbacher Gourmet Popcorn is made with top 20% corn, which pops lighter and fluffier, with fewer unpopped kernels than competition. Popcorn is a good source of dietary fiber.	
Consumer benefit	A healthy alternative to chips plus best-quality popcorn that I deserve.	Easy to make and always tastes great. I can share with my friends.
Emotional benefit	I don't feel guilty about indulging on a snack.	Orville makes parties and time with friends more fun.

ing for the car or the insurance or both, may be attracted to it because it is affordable and durable. It is the same car, but there are two very different motivations for choosing a Honda Civic.

How do we deal with this in rolling up our benefit ladder? After doing the laddering exercise, it is also wise to build a benefit matrix. A benefit matrix is a template you can use to account for differing target markets. You may have a matrix that includes different demographic groups, mind-sets, or behaviors. The example in Table 12.5 is a simple benefit matrix for Orville Redenbacher popcorn. The two target markets are moms and 'tween girls (ages 8 to 12).

Unlike benefit laddering, where the target market is the foundation of the pyramid, in the matrix you create columns listing target markets. The one row that remains constant in the matrix is the product attributes of the brand. In this case, Orville Redenbacher popcorn has some unique attributes with regard to how it is made.

As you can see, while the product attributes are the same, these two consumer groups have different reasons for using it. For mom, the popcorn brand taps into her need to feed her kids healthy snacks. She would much rather have her kids eat popcorn than chips or other items. She doesn't feel guilty about letting her kids munch a bunch of popcorn. 'Tween girls, on the other hand, could care less about eating healthy, but they do care about what their friends think of them, particularly when they are having a sleepover. For this group, Orville Redenbacher does a couple of things. First, it is a snack that kids can make themselves so they feel empowered. Second, it is fun and makes sharing a good time. It is a social event for a group that can sometimes have social phobias.

Figure 12.2 **Brand Wheel Example: Malibu Rum**

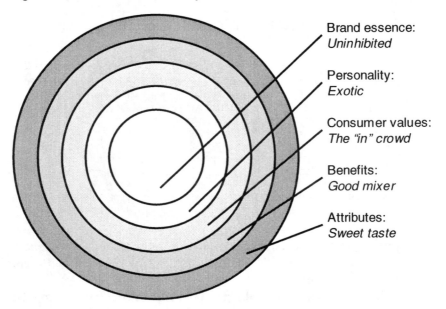

Brand essence:
Uninhibited

Personality:
Exotic

Consumer values:
The "in" crowd

Benefits:
Good mixer

Attributes:
Sweet taste

Now that you have analyzed the brand's attributes and benefits and have compared it to other brands, it is time to develop the brand's essence. The brand's essence is a one- or two-word summary of all the work that you have put into clarifying the brand's position. It is like the "elevator speech," the quick two-minute message, for the brand. Or it is the summary of how a movie is pitched. For example, Star Trek was initially pitched as a "space Western." That was the "essence" of the story.

To get to a brand's essence, it is valuable to use a brand essence wheel like the one illustrated in Figure 12.2. The brand essence wheel consists of the outer ring of brand attributes, a second ring of brand benefits, a third ring of consumer values, a fourth ring of the brand's personality, and finally the brand's essence.

Let's take a look at an example for Malibu rum. This coconut-flavored rum comes in a white bottle and has a sweet taste. These are examples of the brand's attributes. They are the building blocks of the brand.

This leads to the benefits of Malibu rum. It is a good mixer. It is easy to drink. As a result, it is very popular rum that can ladder up to feeling like you are a part of the party.

This leads to the consumer value. Here we are describing who the brand appeals to and what they want and how it fits into their lives. Malibu rum is a drink for the "in" crowd or popular group. It makes their lives more fun.

This leads to the brand's personality. Malibu rum is accessible yet exotic and sexy.

This leads to the brand essence of "Uninhibited Caribbean Fun." That is what Malibu rum is all about.

The brand's essence becomes a shorthand for describing the brand. Rather than providing a full brand positioning statement, a brand essence boils it down to a few words. This is a great exercise that provides a way to translate brand positioning for a creative department so they keep the brand essence in mind when they are developing advertising.

Summary

Defining the brand's essence is one of the most important aspects of being an account planner. To get to the heart of the brand, it is important to understand that any company is devoted to building unique features or attributes into their brand. These attributes are the cornerstone of their business. However, the trick is to turn those attributes into consumer benefits. Your role is to help guide the brand from defining the functional benefit of the brand to a more powerful emotional benefit. You should work to help the brand understand how it fits into a consumer's life and define the consumer values that a brand can tap into to make that consumer's life better. Then it is your job to boil down all these items into a few simple words that capture the essence of the brand. That will help set into motion all of the communications that will further the brand's cause.

Review Questions

1. What are the differences between attributes and benefits? How do attributes help an advertiser? How do benefits help an advertiser?
2. What kinds of products and services make use of sensory attributes?
3. What are possible attributes for automobiles, retail stores, liquid cleansers, television sets, and pest-control services?
4. What are the possible benefits of each of these categories? Work from functional benefits to emotional benefits, then sum up a brand essence.

Discussion Questions

1. Analyze the higher order on the benefit ladder. What are the advantages of the higher positions? What are the disadvantages?

2. Analyze the functional, emotional, and sensory characteristics of products and services. What are the advantages of each? What are the disadvantages?
3. Analyze a brand positioning statement compared to a brand essence. What are the similarities?

Additional Resources

Bedbury, S., and S. Fenichell, S. *A New Brand World: Eight Principles for Achieving Brand Leadership in the Twenty-First Century.* Middlesex, England: Penguin, 2003.

Ries, A., and L. Ries. *22 Immutable Laws of Branding: How to Build a Product or Service into a World-Class Brand.* New York: Collins Business, 2002.

13

What Is a Big Idea?

Isn't coming up with the Big Idea what advertising is all about? While big ideas are what the advertising business is built on, when you ask advertising professionals and students about a big idea, you may get a variety of responses. Most people will cite some form of creative execution. Usually, it is a "Wow that is really cool!" or "That is really funny" or "That was great." Some people will cite certain copy or a tagline. Others may cite a moving scene or a particular piece of music.

When pressed to define a "big idea," most advertising professionals and students cite specific advertising campaigns. Some mention the campaigns for Apple. Others cite Geico as their favorite. Regardless of the product, advertising campaigns are usually associated with a big idea.

Executions of individual advertisements and even great advertising campaigns are not big ideas in and of themselves. Advertising is merely means to express an idea. In his book, *Ogilvy on Advertising*, David Ogilvy says "Unless your campaign contains a big idea, it will pass like a ship in the night." We all know that getting to a big idea is important. It is the lifeblood of your advertising campaign. Now that we know what it is not, let's discuss what a big idea is.

The Big Idea?

So what is a big idea? We define an advertising big idea as the central idea of the campaign. It is the one thing that is the key consumer takeaway from all research, discussion, and creativity that goes into an advertising campaign.

Well-conceived big ideas can be expressed in a single sentence. They are broad enough to encompass any creative execution. They are simple and are the result of an insight. As we discussed previously, that insight can be generated by the category, advertising, or consumer.

Imagine that you wanted to market casual pants to men in an era when men only wore suits to work. You initially positioned them as weekend pants or as pants for all occasions. But it was tough to get men to trade in their jeans for casual pants so you were stuck. Men wore suits to work and jeans on the weekend. How could you bust through? That was the situation that Dockers and its agency at the time, Goodby, Silverstein & Partners, faced. The idea they used to bust through was simple. Dockers created "casual Fridays," the one day when men didn't have to wear a suit to work. They could wear slacks and Dockers happened to be the slacks of choice. Now that was a big idea. It is not an advertising idea but it is a big idea. It actually transformed the modern workplace.

Now that we are getting warmed up, let's take a look at big ideas in advertising. The Ad Council has a history of coming up with some big ideas. They use big ideas to change longstanding dangerous consumer behaviors. They work to reduce smoking and combat drunken driving and teenage drinking to name a few. Their campaign to tackle drunken driving shows what a big idea can do. Through research, the Ad Council found that most consumers seemed to know when they were drunk. To the majority of consumers, being drunk meant drinking four or more drinks and/or having slurred speech, wobbly legs, and blurred vision. Who would want to drive when they felt that way? The answer was no one. However, the problem is that a few drinks impair your ability behind the wheel. The insight that the Ad Council found was that most consumers drank to get "buzzed" or a bit happy. Armed with that insight, the big idea was to redefine drunken driving: "Buzzed driving = drunken driving." The results of the campaign were startling. By reframing the way consumers viewed drunken driving, they were much more likely to not drive even after just a few drinks.

MasterCard created its well known "Priceless" advertising campaign. Who hasn't laughed at some of the situations that the advertising agency uses to dramatize what is "priceless." While the Priceless campaign is an award-winning one, it comes from a simple big idea. The big idea behind the campaign is "The best way to pay for everything that matters." The expression of that big idea is "Priceless."

In Jean-Marie Dru's book *Beyond Disruption,* he describes how TWBA/Chiat/Day looks at developing a disruptive big idea. TBWA/Chiat/Day's method for this is called disruption. Basically, the idea is to find what is common in the category and take an opposing viewpoint. TBWA/Chiat/Day calls it finding conventions. This disruption process is a forum for insights. From there a new vision or idea is generated that leads to a disruption in the category.

One of the agency's classic cases is Apple Computer, Inc. The conven-

Figure 13.1 **Example of a Dove Ad**

Do you believe that real beauty comes in many shapes and sizes?

Join the Campaign   campaignforrealbeauty.com

tion or insight is that in high-technology products, communication usually revolves around product features and benefits. It is largely about the computer and not about the user. The user was typically seen as a nerd; someone who is very analytical and not very artistic. The big idea was that Apple could be a tool for creative minds. The execution of that idea was transforming the computer into a value statement about being creative and paying homage to those who are creative thinkers.

Dove is another example of a recent award-winning campaign. Research showed that the majority of women did not think they were beautiful. Women were tested on a battery of self-esteem questions before and after reading fashion and beauty magazines. The results showed that after reading magazines filled with fashion models, women had lower self-esteem. They felt there was no way they could measure up. That led to the insight that beauty has been defined by narrow stereotypes.

The big idea was that "real beauty comes in many shapes, sizes and ages" (see Figure 13.1). It led to a campaign that redefines what beauty means. It allowed consumers to get into the act and help define beauty. The Web site for the campaign, campaignforrealbeauty.com, became a haven for women sharing their stories.

Figure 13.2   **The Steps to a Big Idea**

togetherness
strategy

FLORIDA IS THE CONNECTOR

FOR RELATIONSHIP TRAVELERS TO

SHARE EXPERIENCES

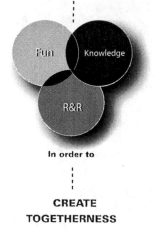

In order to

**CREATE
TOGETHERNESS**

The NSAC award-winning campaign for Florida Tourism by Southern Methodist University is a good example of a student team that came up with a big idea. The insight was that most travel advertising featured the destination. White sandy beaches, sunny days, and great nightlife were the usual topics of the ads. However, travelers talked more about their experiences than the destination itself. All this led to the big idea of "Florida is the leisure travel investment that creates togetherness." That idea was captured in the tagline, "This is family. This is Florida." The idea of the campaign was to demonstrate family fun that creates lasting memories (Figure 13.2).

A big idea is the main message or theme that holds any form of communication together. When creating award-winning campaigns, there are two fundamentals: Coming up with a big idea and coming up with a dramatic expression of that idea. The expression of the idea is how to say it and where to say it. It encompasses all facets of the campaign.

Finding and Pitching Big Ideas

Now that you know what a big idea is and what it isn't, how do you come up with big ideas and how do you pitch them?

In *A Technique for Producing Ideas,* James Webb Young describes an idea as "nothing more nor less than a new combination of old elements." When you stop and think about it, that is exactly what an idea is. It is the unexpected joining of two "old elements" to create a new "whole," or new idea or thought.

Johannes Gutenberg put a coin punch and a wine press together and got a printing press. Levi Hutchins put an alarm and a clock together and got an alarm clock. Steve Jobs and his company, Apple, put together a computer and a phone to get the iPhone. If you think about most products, they are the concrete expression of an idea.

There are numerous books and articles that give advice on how to get an idea. It usually boils down to a few simple steps. In the book *How to Get Ideas,* Jack Foster offers some examples of how various philosophers and scientists arrived at new thoughts.

For example, Hermann von Helmholtz, the German philosopher, used a three-step process: (1) preparation, the time during which one investigates the problem; (2) incubation, when one doesn't think consciously about the problem; and (3) illumination, when ideas come unexpectedly and without effort.

Moshe F. Rubinstein, a specialist in scientific problem solving, offers up four steps: preparation, incubation, inspiration, and verification.

James Webb Young, the former copywriter at JWT (the current name for the former J. Walter Thompson advertising agency), has a five-step process for producing ideas. The first step is to gather specific knowledge about the products, people, and general knowledge about life and events. The second step is to go through a process of masticating those materials. The third step is to drop the subject and rest. The fourth is where an idea will appear. And the fifth is where you take your idea out into the world.

Regardless of the steps, the process is basically the same. You do your homework, put new combinations of things together, and then you test your idea in the marketplace.

No other industry is more dependent on big ideas than the entertainment industry. Pitching a movie is just like pitching an advertising idea. Movie executives expect the screenwriter to be able to sum up the idea in a sentence. In fact, the unwritten rule of a good movie is that if you can't explain it in eight words or less, then it isn't a good idea. And most movie ideas are unexpected combinations of old ideas, just as James Webb Young said about advertising.

For example, *E.T.* was about a cuddly alien who wanted to find his mother. Until *E.T.* came out, all alien movies had been about horrific creatures who wanted to wreak havoc on the earth or take it over. *E.T.* was about a cute alien who had lost his way.

The movie *Star Trek* was initially pitched as a "space western." The television show *Seinfeld* was a story about "nothing." And the movie *Night at the Museum* is about museum artifacts coming to life. All are simple ideas that can take on a variety of story lines and characters.

When thinking about pitching a big idea, it is a good exercise to practice pitching movie ideas. It is a good warm-up for pitching your "big idea" to the client.

Six Strategies for Communicating

Sometimes coming up with a big idea can be overwhelming. There seem to be endless ideas in the advertising universe. However, advertising is based upon a few fundamental appeals. In his book *The Psychology of Persuasion,* Robert Cialdini discusses six overarching appeals that have been proven to be persuasive. These six appeals are at the center of most successful advertising campaigns and ideas.

1. Reciprocity

The first appeal is reciprocity. Reciprocity is based on the simple idea that if I give you something, you will want to give me something. This simple idea is the basis for any promotional offer. If I give you a $1.00-off coupon, you will buy my product. Or if I allow you to buy one and get another free, that is also an example of reciprocity. But reciprocity can take on a bigger campaign meaning. The Progressive insurance company uses this idea in their award-winning campaign. They provide an easy way for you to compare auto insurance with the understanding that you will select theirs.

2. Commitment

The second appeal is commitment. This idea is based on having the consumer do something with your brand. In doing something, they become committed. For example, if you get to drive a new car over the weekend, the chances are great that you will buy it. Doritos asked consumers to submit an idea for a television commercial that would be aired during the Super Bowl. What a great way of using consumer-generated ideas to gain commitment to the brand.

3. Social Proof

The third appeal is a mainstay of the advertising business. It is social proof: If everyone else is buying it, it must be the best choice. Social proof uses the peer group as a frame of reference. Claims such as "fastest growing," "most popular," or "prefer us 2 to 1" are all examples of social proof. Thumb through a women's fashion magazine and you will see many examples of social proof.

4. Liking

The fourth appeal is another pillar of advertising: liking. It is no secret that just like people, brands that are well liked are preferred over brands that are not well liked. Ads that are well liked perform better than ads that are not well liked. The idea is to find some association that the consumer will like. It may be a celebrity or a puppy or an animated character. If it is likeable, then it has a good chance of succeeding.

5. Directed Reference

The fifth appeal is directed reference. This is embodied by an authority figure, usually an expert. For example, nearly every pharmaceutical ad has a man in a lab coat posing as a doctor or an authority figure. Allstate Insurance uses a famous actor who starred in an action series. He embodies the company taking care of you.

6. Scarcity

The sixth appeal is scarcity. Scarcity is a time-honored marketing technique. The limited-time offer is a key marketing ploy. This deal is only available for a short time so you had better take advantage of it now. There are only a few left, so act now! Scarcity is a classic strategy for big ideas. The most famous is the initial campaign for the California Milk Processor Board that resulted in the "Got Milk?" campaign. The original idea was "to persuade people to buy more milk by reminding them of the horrors of running out of it."

These six persuasion strategies are hallmarks of the advertising and marketing world. Many award-winning campaigns are built on these simple, time-tested strategies.

What Makes an Award-Winning Campaign

Throughout this book, we discuss what makes an award-winning campaign. Our examples from both professional award campaigns and student campaigns have many things in common. When you survey any award-winning advertising, whether it's a campaign or created for specific media such as the Kelly awards for print or OBIE awards for out-of-home advertising, it boils down to a few simple items.

The first is that you must have a big idea. Without a big idea, you will not have anything that is memorable. A big advertising idea must be both original and relevant. This leads us to the second aspect of an award-winning campaign: connecting in a relevant and emotional way; it must yield an intense response.

The third aspect of a great campaign is some form of unexpected consistency. The execution is unexpected but consistent, continuing the theme in novel ways, so that it isn't just a sight gag. There were a number of unexpected ads during the dot-com heydays of the early 2000s, yet most were just one-offs and not full campaigns. Yet finding the unexpected is a central tenet to the relationship between success and failure of a brand. Studies from the IPC show that "brand fame" is the single best correlation for brand success. That means that the more people talk about your brand at the water cooler, the more likely it is to become a commercial success. That is why there are a lot of attempts in advertising to do the outrageous. Finding something unexpected that transcends a single moment is the trick to finding long-lasting success.

In the book *A Master Class in Brand Planning: The Timeless Works of Stephen King,* Mr. King places creative execution ideas into two main camps: Those that rely on a vivid demonstration to make their point and those that rely on a vivid metaphor. These two methods plus a combination of the two are the three methods of creative execution.

Much advertising is based on a product feature or benefit demonstration. A vivid demonstration restates an old truth. Vivid demonstrations are usually based on picking a specific attribute and feature of a brand and demonstrating it as better than the competition.

The Verizon cellular service campaign is built on the benefit of a larger coverage area. To demonstrate this, the ads put people in "dead zones" where they are saved by the Verizon army and its chief (the "Can you hear me now" man). This is a great example of a vivid demonstration and the use of a vivid metaphor.

Another classic example of a vivid demonstration using a vivid metaphor is the Apple versus PC campaign. In these simple executions, the Apple spokesperson is watching the comical PC metaphor struggle to get the best of Apple.

Both campaigns have clear big ideas. They connect in an emotional manner and they are consistent in their use of vivid demonstration and vivid metaphor. Their series of commercials can go on for a long time. They have a consistent format and, much like a situation comedy, each "episode" is fresh and new.

Vivid metaphors are based on a brand's personality. A metaphor borrows something outside the brand that may have similar personality characteristics or attributes that can be associated with the brand.

There are classic examples of vivid metaphors in many award-winning campaigns.

The Geico caveman campaign is an example of a vivid metaphor. "So easy a caveman can do it," sums up the ease and simplicity of using Geico's online method of buying auto insurance. It pays off the overall position of "15 minutes can save you 15 percent." The Marlboro Man is a vivid metaphor for what Marlboro stands for. He symbolizes the rugged, individualistic man that we associate with the brand. The "Most interesting man in the world" campaign for Dos Equis beer is another example of a vivid metaphor.

It is not important to define your campaign as a vivid demonstration or a vivid metaphor. However, if you don't have either, you are likely not to have an award-winning campaign.

In summary, to develop an award-winning campaign, you need to come up with a big idea. A big idea is not the creative execution; it is the single takeaway that comes from all of the expressions of that idea and it should be communicated in a single sentence. Based on the big idea, it is time to find a memorable way to express it. This can be done either by a vivid demonstration or a vivid metaphor. Regardless of the approach, the creative needs to be relevant and unexpected. It must connect in an emotional way to its audience. With all of this tied with a neat bow, you will have the makings of an award-winning campaign.

Review Questions

1. What is the definition of a big idea? How is it different from an advertising campaign?
2. How can you use the six communication strategies?
3. What makes an award-winning campaign?
4. What are the key aspects of developing an award-winning creative execution?

Discussion Questions

1. Can you develop an award-winning advertising campaign without a big idea?

2. What is the difference between a big idea and an advertising idea?
3. How do you come up with big ideas?

Additional Resources

Barry, P. *The Advertising Concept Book.* New York: Thames & Hudson, 2008.
Foster, J. *How to Get Ideas.* San Francisco: Berrett-Koehler, 2006.
Lois, G. *George Lois on His Creation of the Big Idea.* New York: Assouline, 2008.

14

Briefing the Team to Get a Great Campaign

You've done your research. You have worked to position the product properly. You have a big idea that will help set the brand apart from the competition. All of that hard work is for naught unless you can properly tell the story. It is the creative expression of the big idea that separates a strategically sound yet mundane campaign from an award-winning campaign.

To make the big idea come to life, you need to properly brief the agency. That is one of the most important aspects of account planning. You are the focal point for briefing the entire agency team on what direction the campaign must take. Account planners take a great amount of pride in the way they brief the team. Developing a brief is the one tangible product that they produce. And it is a very visible product to the agency employees and the client. It becomes their roadmap to success.

In today's highly fragmented media world, the briefing process takes on even greater importance than it did twenty or thirty years ago when there was a much more limited number of media outlets. The creative strategy is "what to say." The creative execution is "how to say it." Both are crucial to the success of the campaign. However, the contact portion of the campaign has taken on increasing importance. So "where to say it" or "how to connect with the consumer" now has equal billing in the campaign strategy.

Much of creative strategy development uses what psychologists refer to as convergent thinking. This is the process of drawing deductive and logical conclusions from the information at hand. It progresses from general to specific. This is an informational part of the process. Convergent thinking is used to distill the essence of the problem and to decide which particular piece of information or imagery will change the consumer's perception and behavior. Thus, it is a crucial part of developing the agency brief. It is this process of distillation that leads to the big idea, a focused single thought.

Once a brief is fully developed, we enter into another phase of thinking called divergent thinking. This style of thinking goes from specific to general or from the specific instances and situations to generalizations. This style of thinking is used by advertising creative departments to devise advertising campaigns that will present the idea or imagery in a fresh new way.

While it is a popular myth that creative directors are rebels who are undisciplined creative artists who don't pay attention to strategy, this couldn't be farther from the truth. The truth is that creative directors not only embrace great strategy derived from a briefing document, they demand it.

There is nothing more frustrating to a creative director than a loose or undeveloped strategy. "Give me the freedom of a tight strategy" is a mantra heard at many advertising agencies. The tighter the strategy, the more specific the big idea, the more the creative team can stretch their minds to find an unusual way to communicate it. Again, because the stakes are high and the media landscape is so fragmented, the creative strategy must be crystal clear and it must inspire the creative team.

The issue of fragmentation has led to formation of multi-disciplinary teams that can include account management, media, digital, public relations, social media, and the creative team. In the past, an advertising agency's brief was just a creative brief delivered to the writer and art director team who worked on the account. This process worked fairly well when everyone knew that television was the lead medium with print and radio as support vehicles. However, in today's world there are a multitude of choices for paid media advertising and an equally daunting array of choices in the social and digital media arena that are not paid media.

While the media landscape has changed, the basic components of delivering a communication strategy with a big idea have remained constant. It boils down to having a compelling message, an equally compelling way to say it, and a convincing way to connect it with consumers.

Early Creative Briefs: Young and Rubicam

Until the developments of the past decade, the creative brief was just that: a statement pertaining only to the creative message. It was used to develop advertising. It was typically developed in the United States by an account executive and delivered to the writer and art director. Today, we know that account planners are largely the authors of agency briefs and that the subject of a brief involves a wide range of departments within the advertising agency.

It is important to understand the early history of the creative brief to see

Figure 14.1   **Y&R Style Creative Brief (Pace Picante Sauce Example)**

Key Fact

70 percent of consumers think of Pace Picante sauce for chips and dips while only 10 percent think of it as an ingredient for everyday cooking.

Problem that Advertising Must Solve

Women are always seeking ways to make their meals more interesting yet they are not aware that Pace could be an ingredient to help them do this.

Advertising Objective

Convince consumers that Pace can be used in a variety off ways to make everyday meals more interesting.

Target Market

Suburban housewives with children who are constantly on the go.

Creative Strategy

Demonstrate that Pace can add zest to everyday recipes such as meatloaf, soup, or casseroles.

how advertising has evolved. In its simplest form, a creative brief delivers three pieces of information:

- To whom are you directing the message (target market)
- Of what are you trying to convince them
- Why they should believe it

Much of the early creative briefing documents came directly from brand positioning statements (see Chapter 10).

In fact, some of the early creative briefs used in the 1960s and 1970s did not contain any more questions than were just listed. These early creative briefs were linear in terms of the thinking involved. Most of the documents were designed to emphasize functional product benefits. The 1960s and 1970s were the heyday of new products that contained unique product attributes that could be turned into benefits.

The majority of early creative briefs were greatly influenced by the advertising agency Young & Rubicam (Y&R). The Y&R style of creative brief had five elements that worked in a sequential fashion. Figure 14.1 is an example of this style of creative brief.

This brief begins with a key fact. The key fact is the distillation of the research available on the brand and the market. It should be the one fact that is most relevant to the advertising of the given brand at the given time. There could be facts that are more compelling from a marketing perspective such as a loss of distribution or a weakness in the commodity market but those aren't key facts for a creative brief.

Another way to look at the key fact is that it sums up the situation. For example, in the case of Pace Picante sauce, the key fact was that 70 percent of consumers thought of Pace only as a dip for chips. Based on that key fact, you begin to see that the marketing problem is to broaden the brand's usage appeal.

The second part of the brief is defining the problem that advertising must solve. The statement of the problem should be related to the key fact but it must be stated in terms of the consumer. There is a real temptation to state the problem based on what the brand needs. But what the brand needs belongs in the marketing plan and what the consumer needs belongs in the creative brief.

In this case, the consumer problem was that women associated Pace with just serving chips and dips at party time but not for regular cooking. Yet women were always seeking ways of making their day-to-day meals more interesting.

The third aspect of the creative brief is the advertising objective. The objective is what you are trying to accomplish. In this case, the objective is to convince women that Pace can be used in a variety of ways to make their everyday meals more interesting.

The fourth aspect is the target consumer. This is who we are addressing and what they are really like. This definition can include demographics as well as psychographics or lifestyle characteristics. In the case of Pace Picante sauce, the target is defined as suburban housewives who are constantly on the go.

The fifth and most important part of the creative brief is the creative strategy itself. What do we want to say? This connects the problem with the solution. The creative strategy in our example is to demonstrate other ways that housewives can use Pace sauce.

Finally, the creative brief contains the tone or personality of the brand. For advertising, it is the feeling or mood that you want to encompass. For Pace, the personality was lively, a bit irreverent, and fun.

This iterative process was driven largely by the clients that dominated the scene at Y&R, which was known as an agency for consumer packaged-goods accounts. As a result, the process was very linear and was correlated with the brand-positioning document that the brand presented to the agency team.

The fundamental building blocks of great communication certainly rest in these early documents. The key breakthrough in these documents was the stating of a consumer problem. Prior to these documents, advertising professionals were given marketing plans and asked to help the brand solve their problem. By turning the problem on its head, it began to force marketers to

Figure 14.2   **Leo Burnett Brief: Tide Example**

- **Convince (Who):** Cost-conscious moms of large blue-collar families with active children who wash clothes so frequently that they wear them out.
- **That (What belief or benefit):** Tide gets clothes their cleanest and keeps them looking new.
- **Because (Why-reasons-support):** Tide's formulation powers out stains while keeping clothes from fading or fraying and it is trusted and endorsed by the Cotton Association.

see the world from a different perspective. This helped lead the charge of much better and compelling creative.

Leo Burnett Brief

Another early brief that has survived the test of time came from Leo Burnett. Burnett was also known as a very strong consumer packaged-goods agency based out of Chicago. This agency was also known as the "critter" agency for developing brand icons such as Jolly Green Giant, Tony the Tiger, and the Marlboro Man, just to mention a few.

The Burnett brief boiled the process down to three steps. Figure 14.2 shows an example of a Burnett brief. The initial step is to define the target. In this case, Burnett puts it as an objective, "to convince." In the example of Tide, it is to convince cost-conscious moms of active families. The initial part of the brief serves the beginning of the objective.

The second part of the brief is "that," which is what we want the consumer to believe. This forms the basis for the creative strategy. In this case, Tide wants to convince cost-conscious moms that Tide will get clothes clean as well as keep them looking new.

The final aspect is "because." This is the reason why or support behind what you are trying to convince the consumer about. In the case of Tide, the reason why is that their special formula not only cleans clothes but keeps them from fading or fraying, and that is what keeps them looking new longer.

The Burnett brief is a distillation of the brand positioning statement. It forces a very strong point of view. As a result, it provides very clear direction to the creative team.

Project Brief

Creative briefs were designed to be campaign briefs. They provided overall direction for a campaign but not the specifics. Early creative briefs largely assumed that television would be the dominant medium. That was the case in the mid to late part of the twentieth century.

Figure 14.3   **Typical Project Creative Brief**

Question	Answer
What are we advertising?	Description of the product including all pertinent facts
Whom are we talking to?	Description of target audience
What is the objective?	Description of what the advertising is attempting to achieve
Where is the advertising running?	Schedule of media including types and sizes
What is the creative strategy?	A description of the selling proposition with rationale and copy points on product features and benefits
What else do we need to include in the advertising?	List of mandatories to be included, and list of items not to be included
When is the deadline?	Dates to review concepts and executions

The project brief was developed to provide direction for individual ads or specific projects within a campaign. Figure 14.3 provides an example of a typical creative project brief that agencies use today.

The project brief contains a pragmatic view of the advertising process. It begins with a description of the product or service being advertised, including any pertinent facts about it. Then it moves to a brief discussion of the target market. The third point is the advertising objective, discussing what the advertising is designed to achieve. The fourth point is when the discussion of media types and sizes that should be used in the campaign is added to the equation. This is something that earlier creative briefs did not address. The fifth point is the creative strategy. This is a description of the selling proposition, including the details on rationale and copy points. The sixth and seventh points are the most pragmatic. They include a list of mandatory items or "must haves." These may include legal copy or any other items that are essential in ad. Finally, there is a discussion of due dates for the initial concept work and for the final execution of the ads.

Contemporary Brief

Creative briefing has changed over time and the creative brief itself has changed with it. One of the big changes is that the creative brief needs to

Tabe 14.1

Contemporary Brief

1. What is the problem?
2. Whom are we marketing to?
3. What do they currently think and do?
4. What do want them to think and do?
5. What is the idea that will get them to think that way?
6. What are the best ways to connect the idea to the consumer?
7. What tone do we want to take?
8. How will we measure success?
9. What are the mandatories and key milestones?

direct the creative team, a digital team, a media team, a public relations team, and perhaps a marketing services team. As a result, the brief needs to include broad thoughts on how to reach the target market as well as what message will best motivate the target market.

Another thing that has changed in the United States is the state of most consumer categories. The United States is a very mature market for many consumer goods. As a result, there are many brands and categories where there is little product differentiation. This has led to much more focus on developing an emotional benefit difference rather than a functional benefit difference. Most initial creative briefs were developed when functional benefits were the mainstay of advertising and brands tended to have unique points of difference. But in today's parity landscape, marketers rely on emotional differences to separate one brand from another.

The other aspect of the contemporary brief is that it includes a discussion on accountability. It is important to know not only what success looks like but how to measure it. This becomes increasingly important as success is measured by behavior as well as changes in attitudes toward a brand. As more agencies and clients develop compensation programs that have a part of the compensation based on brand performance, it is in everyone's best interest to agree on how to measure success.

Now let's take a look at an example of a contemporary brief and walk through each aspect of it (see Table 14.1).

What Is the Problem?

The first part of the brief is to state the problem. This is similar to the earlier creative briefs, which stated the problem that advertising must solve. In the contemporary brief, advertising is one of many solutions to the consumer problem, so we don't want to be constrained by traditional thinking. With the changing nature of communications it is a good idea to keep an open mind regarding the solution.

However, just like the other briefs, the problem should be stated in consumer language. While a marketing problem may be that "sales are soft," this is not a consumer problem. We need to know *why* sales are soft. For example, consumers may not be buying as much Dove soap as in the past because they believe that all soaps are the same.

As a part of the problem, it is also good to ask the question, "Why are we advertising?" Or it may be a direct question to a client, "Why are you coming to us to solve your problem?"

These are questions that makes advertising agency management quiver. And as simple as it may seem, often the advertiser and the advertising agency aren't on the same page about it. More than half of the problems that develop between a client and an agency can be traced back to the issue of creative strategy. Put another way, there is often a lack of understanding about just what the advertising is intended to accomplish. So, properly stating the problem and agreeing on it up front is a crucial step toward developing the final advertising campaign.

To Whom Are We Marketing?

As we have discussed, when you describe to whom you are marketing, the description should be more robust than just a list of demographic characteristics. The goal is to paint a succinct picture of the consumer so that whoever is trying to solve the problem can understand the potential consumer.

For example, it is inadequate to just say that your target is women who buy disposable diapers or engineers who specify silicon chips. This tells you who they are but not what they think or feel. This is where you need to draw a broader picture of motivations.

For example, a finicky mom who always wants the best for her child or a senior engineer who strives to be at the leading edge of technology tells you something about how each of these target consumers thinks. This can be thought of as developing a character in a play or on a television show. You need to understand their motivations and the context in which they make decisions.

What Do They Currently Think and Do?

This is where you get inside the consumer's mind and determine what they currently think or believe about the brand and, as a result of that thinking, how they behave. For example, consumers may think that all auto insurance companies are basically the same. As a result of that thinking, they will select the one they feel is the cheapest or the one that they have heard of.

Within this statement you should cover some diagnostic ground. You need to understand the awareness of the brand, preference for the brand, and attitudes toward it. In essence, you are looking to uncover barriers to further adoption of the brand.

What Do We Want Them to Think and Do?

This is the major question. And it also defines your vision of the brand. This is where you craft what you want the outcome of your effort to be. If consumers think of your brand as old and stodgy, then you may have a vision that the brand is now relevant. If consumers aren't considering your brand, then you want them to consider it first.

Crafting a brand vision is not just choosing the opposite of what consumers currently think and do. It is developing a brand destination. The vision has to be realistic yet aspirational. You are looking to change behavior with your campaign and to do that you are likely going to change the consumer's view of the brand.

This part of the briefing process is crucial for you, the account planner, and the client to agree upon. Unless you have a clear direction or destination, it is impossible to develop an idea and execution that will get you there.

What Is the Idea that Will Get Them to Think That Way?

Now is the time to discuss the big idea. This is something that will motivate the consumer to take the course of action that leads to the destination. This is the communication strategy. It could be a key benefit or a new way of looking at the brand. It could be some new information or some new emotional insight. Whatever the nugget, this is where you want to deliver it. This is also the point where you outline the reason why it is a compelling idea.

What Are the Best Ways to Connect the Idea to the Consumer?

This is where you can introduce a discussion about communication channels. Because this brief goes to media, public relations, digital, and other professional communicators, it is important to consider all forms of communication: traditional media vehicles such as television or magazines and nontraditional media such as video games, cell phones, or guerilla activity. There should be a discussion of digital channels and social media as well. The goal of this section of the brief is to stretch the boundaries of how to connect the idea to the consumer.

What Tone Do We Want to Take?

Here you want to reprise what the brand personality is all about. Your communication should reflect what tone you want to use in communicating about the brand. Again, this should be done on an aspirational basis. If the brand is perceived to be old and stodgy the tone should avoid sounding that way. It should be in keeping with the brand personality while always moving it ahead.

How Will We Measure Success?

In this section of the brief, you should discuss how you will measure changes to consumers' perception or thinking about the brand as well as how to measure their behavior.

For a communications campaign, it is crucial to measure both the perception and the behavior of consumers. It is possible to change one and not the other. For example, you could offer an incentive to buy a car, which might change short-term behavior but might not really change the long-term perception of the brand. On the other hand, you might be equally successful by driving people to a dealership to buy a car but it may not be priced appropriately so there will be no sale, because you have changed perception but not final buying behavior.

Regardless of your brand's purchase dynamics and attitudes, this section is crucial to defining how you will proceed with a campaign. Each side of the consumer equation should be taken into account in the measurement of campaign success.

What Are the Mandatories and Key Milestones?

These are two questions that are necessary in the campaign process. Mandatories are items that are required in the campaign, for example, the use of a slogan or an icon or a media sponsorship or certain advertising media buys. The most common mandatories are legal mandatories. These are statements that you must make in any form of advertisement for that brand. Every company has something that falls into this category. If you are working on a pharmaceutical product, you may have a full page of legal disclaimers and mandatory copy. In other categories, there may be just a few, such as trademarks or copyrights. Regardless of what the mandatories are, they must be included in the campaign.

Milestones or a timeline must also be indicated in the brief. Every plan must have due dates. Typically, each step of the process is listed along with a target date of completion.

As you can see, the contemporary brief is much broader than earlier briefs. It is more expansive in the area of strategies, as both creative and media are included in the same brief.

In summary, while briefs have changed over time in response to a more complex marketplace, the fundamentals of good communication remain the same. The remedy for complexity lies in being simple and focused. The communications-briefing document is a way of gaining focus and having the entire agency marching to the beat of the same drummer.

Make the Briefing Come Alive

We have discussed how briefs have changed over time. These changes affect the execution of the brief. In the early days of advertising, a brief was only addressed to the creative department or creative team. In many ways initial briefs were glorified work orders. While briefs were done in a thoughtful manner, they were written and delivered to the creative team as a part of the process. There was not a lot of fanfare in how they were delivered. They were just a matter of fact.

In today's advertising world, an account planner is required to not only write a strategically sound brief but to also use that brief to help inspire great creative work. The same amount of thought that goes into selling the creative brief is applied to actually writing the brief. The "briefing" itself can be as theatrical as the actual advertising that it is intended to generate.

The account planner uses this "briefing platform" to tell the story of the product within the context of the consumer target market. The passion that the account planner has for the strategy will be felt and reflected in the advertising. It is not unlike a coach selling his game plan to his team. If he isn't excited about it, his team will not be too likely to get behind it. The same is true here. The account planner must provide information as well as inspiration.

During the briefing process, it is critical that the account planner achieve three things. The first is to paint a vivid picture of whom the advertising will target. This can be developing personas as we have previously discussed. But it can also mean developing a short video that dramatizes what the target is doing and feeling. Many times these target videos are used both within an advertising agency as well as with the client to gain a feel for the market beyond the static expression. The second is to inspire the team to seek a novel solution to the problem.

This involves presenting the big idea in a new way. Just like dramatizing the target market, the account planner may elect to use a short video to capture the idea. Typically within this setting, the video puts the big idea in context with the competitive set. The big idea is designed to move you outside the mainstream of the category. By dramatizing the idea, the account planner can help inspire his team to reach for an unusual solution. The other aspect of inspiration may be to offer some thought starters on ways to break out from the pack. The role of the account planner is to champion creativity. The more you offer the team, the better the end product will be.

The third is to use the briefing as quality control for ideas. You and members of your team will be the arbiters of the final creative product. For creative to be effective, it must not only be distinctive but must be on strategy.

The brief and briefing process is central to creating an award-winning campaign. The tighter the brief the better the end result. And the more drama you can put into bringing the brief to life, the greater the level of enthusiasm will be for the campaign.

Review Questions

1. How have briefs changed over time? Why have they changed?
2. Why does a brief need to match up with the overall brand positioning?
3. What does a brief have to do with the advertising message and media strategy?
4. What does the big idea have to do with media?
5. How does a brief differ from a project brief?

Discussion Questions

1. If a marketer has done a good job crafting a marketing plan, why do you need an advertising brief?
2. In preparing advertising messages, why not just begin by writing or designing the advertisement?
3. Is the brief expressed only in words? Can it involve both words and images?

4. How do convergent and divergent thinking relate to the logical
    processes of inductive and deductive reasoning?

Additional Resources

Glazer, B., and D. Kennedy. *Outrageous Advertising That's Outrageously Success-
    ful: Created for the 99% of Small Business Owners Who Are Dissatisfied with
    the Results They Get.* Garden City, NY: Glazer-Kennedy, 2009.
Ogilvy, D. *Confessions of an Advertising Man.* London: Southbank, 2005.
O'Leary, S., and K. Sheehan. *Building Buzz to Beat the Big Boys.* Westport, CT:
    Praeger, 2008.
Parente, D. *Advertising Campaign Strategy.* Florence, KY: Cengage Learning,
    2003.

15

Account Planning and IMC

Whether it is in the professional marketplace or in a student competition, an award-winning campaign is defined by an integrated marketing communication campaign solution. Integrated marketing communication (IMC) includes advertising, digital, promotions, public relations, and guerilla marketing. If all of these channels fail to deliver on the big idea you will have gaps in your communication plan, which will lead to a fragmented effort or a waste of money and resources.

Traditionally, account planning has been associated more with creative development than with reaching consumers through touch points. However, there has been a movement in the advertising, public relations, and digital areas to have account planners or professionals with an account planning bent to work on communication touch point strategy as well as creative strategy.

This movement toward having account planners work with various channel specialists on channel strategy is the result of some fundamental changes in the communications landscape. One rather obvious change is that the number of media options has dramatically escalated because of new and interactive media. Consumers have access to thousands of media alternatives, from legacy media such as print and broadcast to digital media and the convergence of digital and legacy media.

Not wanting to be stuck with outdated formats, legacy media such as outdoor are quickly transforming themselves with digital out-of-home and interactive units where consumers can text to gain access to an array of choices. The out-of-home industry has scoured the universe for interesting ways to intercept consumers, from putting logos on beach sand to tattooing someone's head. Other media such as television are also becoming more interactive and print media has begun to experiment with ideas such as augmented reality and digital ads within standard print copies. The point is that the landscape is rapidly changing. Almost anything can become an advertising medium.

Another fundamental shift is that consumers are more and more in control of their media choices. The days of advertisers just pushing content to consumers are coming to an end. Consumers are now in a position to choose what they want to watch or read and when they want to watch or read it. The digital revolution that is sweeping across the media industry is allowing consumers to fundamentally shift from passive spectators to active participants.

Another fundamental shift is that the lines between areas in the communication industry are blurring. Media specialists, public relations professionals, and digital marketers were once in separate silos. These areas still contain specialists but these individuals are increasingly coming together to develop integrated plans. In the United States this trend is led by the large media companies that have spun out of the advertising agencies and wield considerable power over the communications industry marketplace.

For award-winning cases in the IPA, Account Planning Awards, or the NSAC student competition, the need to develop an integrated marketing communication campaign is paramount. All of the elements of the campaign must work together for a campaign to be successful. Account planning can play an important role in helping to make this happen.

Role of Account Planning Within IMC

With all the ongoing change in media channels, the role of the account planner has been heightened within the channel-planning or media-buying world. The role of the account planner in IMC planning is to help the team gain insight into the target audience.

Account planners can be helpful in gaining an understanding touch points that are most relevant and meaningful to the audience within the context of the brand. They can also help focus on which channels and methods will best engage a particular consumer. Research has shown that engaging the audience with their "permission" is a much more effective way to build a deeper relationship between the brand and the consumer than by thrusting a message in front of them.

Within the realm of the agency media department, the role of the account planner is to bring a consumer perspective to media. Media teams are still responsible for helping the client understand how best to allocate resources from a cost efficiency and reach and frequency perspective, but now that engagement is becoming more important, the role of account planning has increased within media circles.

The account planner helps media teams dimensionalize the target market and add insight into where the consumer might be the most open to receiving a brand message. The same can be said of the role of account planning within public relations and digital teams.

Figure 15.1   **Right-Hand Ring**

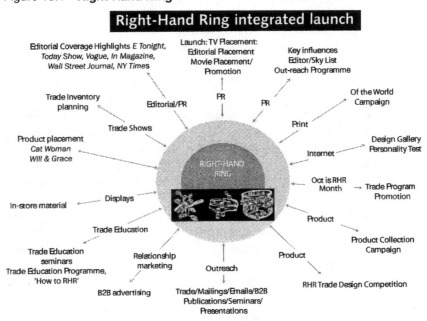

Right-Hand Ring integrated launch

A great example of an integrated campaign launch is found in the IPA DeBeers diamonds campaign. The DeBeers "right hand" strategy was to help grow the diamond market from wedding and engagement rings to jewelry that celebrates relationships. The right-handed ring was positioned as a celebration of the woman who receives it. It is the difference between the left hand, which says "we," and the right hand, which says "me."

The communications in the DeBeers campaign followed a multichannel strategy with the heart of the launch being led by public relations followed by advertising and trade support. Figure 15.1 shows the "right-hand ring integrated launch" schematic. Each touch point of the integrated launch meets a specific need and is based on a specific insight.

The essence of account planning within the communications planning arena is to work with the entire team on reaching the target market. Let's take a look at this key area, where account planning can make a large impact.

Campaign Linkage

Much of a campaign's success comes from linking the big idea to the creative execution through the contact plan. It does little good if the big idea is executed poorly. And it is just as damaging if the big idea isn't reflected in the overall media plan. If the creative team is executing a plan to expand the market with new users but the media team is designing a plan to talk to the brand's existing users, then you will have a disconnect. Although this may seem like a "no brainer," it happens every day. In many instances the creative, media, public relations, and digital teams may all work for separate companies. So the brand manager must ensure that everyone is on the same page. Even when these various disciplines are within the same company or organization, they often have little contact with each other. Or if they do, they can become territorial about their specific turf.

This is where good account planners can earn their keep. The account planner can be the bridge between these various disciplines. The account planner should work in concert with the brand team to ensure that every area that touches the brand's stakeholders is consistent with the message and appropriately conveys the big idea. The account planner can add insights into each area so that everyone is operating with the same level of consumer knowledge.

Melding Target Markets

The key reason is that the account planner should be thoroughly knowledgeable about the target market, which is the key tenet to bringing everyone together. This goal of bringing people together may seem like a simple task but each area has its own nuances.

- The media team typically uses demographics for targeting since they form much of the currency for broadcast and print media.
- The digital team may use behavioral targeting since online advertising is often determined by behavior.
- The public relations team might focus on an editorial target that will influence the consumer rather than on the consumer directly.

These teams will have various ideas of whom or what to target. It is up to the account planner to help guide them to the right target. The key for the account planner is to demonstrate how the target market should work for each area. Let's take a look at offline and online media.

A media team could target women aged 35 to 54 with an HHI $75,000+ for a new brand of cooking ingredient. The digital team could target women who have visited cooking Web sites. However, suppose that the true target is "women who are adventurous cooks." That could bring a whole new meaning to the team.

If the media team is evaluating magazines based on the demographic target they may consider large publications such as *Good Housekeeping* or

Figure 15.2   **Target Considerations: Manwich Sloppy Joe Mix**

Target Considerations Manwich Sloppy Joe Mix		
Target Considerations		**Media Implications**
Women 25-54, w/kids, national	➡	National TV plan
Purchase is in grocery channel with Wal-Mart dominant distributor	➡	Review WalMart TV network or parking lot boards
Moms view Manwich as fun meal with family	➡	Look at "Funtime" TV shows with entire family viewing
Finding Manwich in store can be daunting task	➡	Look at testing in-store graphics
Average purchase is every 2 to 3 week with no large seasonal skews	➡	Recency plan makes sense

Family Circle. The digital team may be coming up with broad cooking Web sites that are offshoots from magazines or specific online niches. But the true target may be someone who is going to www.epicurious.com or is reading *Food and Wine* magazine. That may be where the real "foodie" resides.

The point is that the account planner must add some dimension to the target market descriptions so that media teams and the creative groups are in sync. Sometimes this can be as easy as ensuring the target is consistently defined from a user standpoint; heavy, medium, and light usage of the product or service. Other times it is finding the right motivation for the consumer so that the advertisements are placed in the proper context.

The account planner can provide the details necessary for the media team to develop specific media analysis. This includes demographics and usage information as well as consumer motivations. Figure 15.2 demonstrates the impact of consumer insights on the media plan.

A Day in the Life

One exercise that is extremely effective for developing the insights behind an integrated marketing contact strategy is the "day in the life" exercise; it provides a look at a typical day in the life of your consumer. What media do they come in contact with? Where would be a good time to plant the thought behind the brand?

Finding the right time to get a message to the consumer is important. It

Figure 15.3   **Target: Doug**

Time	Media Consumption
6–7 A.M.	Radio for waking up; read paper
7–8 A.M.	Listen to radio on way to work
12–2 P.M.	Check Internet for news
5–6 P.M.	Listen to radio on the drive home
7–9 P.M.	Watch TV
9–10 P.M.	Surf the Internet
10–11 P.M.	Read a magazine
11 P.M.	Go to sleep

requires determining when the consumer is most susceptible to your message, in other words, it is when they are in the mood. For example, a woman might be most susceptible to a cosmetics advertisement when she is applying her makeup in the morning. Putting a sticker on her bathroom mirror would be a very effective media placement.

Why do you think that the majority of fast food restaurants advertise at noon or between 3:00 and 7:00 in the afternoon? It's because that is when people are hungry. It is effective to remind them of your meal solution when they are thinking about a meal.

Sometimes these moments aren't quite so obvious. Account planners can help the team determine when the consumer would be most receptive to a message. It might involve intercepting them at a specific time of day or at a specific place or when they are likely to be with someone special. Figure 15.3 shows an example of a "day in the life," from an NSAC campaign.

Account planning played a huge role in the media activity for Cheer detergent. Cheer wanted to gain share from moms who had messy kids. They were going after heavy users of laundry detergent. Rather than try to outspend the competition, they decided to take their message to where kids got dirty. So they placed their messages at playgrounds, soccer fields, and little league baseball diamonds. Wherever they felt there would be a connection of dirty kid and mom, they placed ads. The result was a remarkable increase in sales in the targeted market. They had found where their target was most receptive to the message.

The day in the life exercise is a great way to decide where to place your message. It allows each discipline to understand its role in the media mix and how to gain synergy among disciplines.

How the Brand Is Bought

Another meaningful exercise to help aid the IMC team is to review the customer journey, or how the customer actually buys the brand. While this may seem like a simple exercise, knowing how the brand is purchased can sometimes be difficult to determine. For example, if the brand is a can of beans, we know it is usually purchased at the grocery store. However, is it usually an impulse purchase or is it a part of an every-other-week ritual? Depending upon the answer, a totally different plan may result.

If the product is a service, does a salesman sell it to the individual or can it be purchased online? Is it something a student buys because it was recommended by a parent? Or have they spent the past six months researching it? Knowing the ins and outs of the purchase process is crucial to the overall IMC plan. This type of information is vital to a media planner who is considering not only how the brand may fit into the consumer's life but how the consumer goes about purchasing it.

This type of information goes well beyond just knowing the product's purchase cycle. The account planner is looking for insights that offer the media planner a story for developing the contact plan.

In-store advertising plays a role in many impulse purchases. Research shows that in-store media such as floor graphics have a large sales impact on categories such as snack foods and beverages, which are often impulse purchases.

Understanding consumer buying patterns has made a fundamental difference in the way auto insurance is purchased and could impact the development of a marketing plan for this service. In the past, insurance company preferences were passed down and made use of an agent network. Today consumers buy insurance by comparing policies online. Knowing this affects which media reaches these consumers.

Understanding how the consumer buys the brand and what goes through their minds when they are buying it is as important to developing a contact plan as it is to crafting a compelling piece of communication. It is the account planner's responsibility to help the team understand where the brand and the consumer come into contact.

The User Experience

Understanding the customer journey began as a method to understand retail shopping habits. It was used to help marketers understand what happens at the point of decision: when a consumer must choose from a variety of products in a certain category. While this remains largely true for many consumer packaged goods, the online marketplace has made a significant change in the customer journey.

If you are buying a car, you are likely to research it online. You may even elect to buy it online rather than face the experience of dealing with a showroom salesman. Categories such as auto insurance are also moving rapidly to the online marketplace. Other products such as a personal computers or software have been purchased online for many years.

Understanding what the consumer experiences online is as important to many brands as what happens when the consumer sees their product on the shelf. Mapping the user experience can be done both qualitatively and quantitatively. There are tools available that help brands learn about consumers' online shopping habits. Many consumers just visit a Web site briefly and leave. Internet tools can record the length of these visits, which is called a bounce rate. Researchers can find out how long someone spent on a site and what specific pages they spent the most time on.

From this information, you can begin to trace how a consumer works with your Web site. Specialists in this area, called user interface analysts, apply account-planning principles to the online experience.

In the digital age, it is important to understand how the consumer accesses your brand. It can be in a retail store, online, or via a mobile device. Or it might be a combination of channels. It is crucial to understand this and to apply contact strategies when the consumer wants to come into contact with your brand.

Efficiency Versus Effectiveness

Media planning is a balancing act between media cost efficiencies and media effectiveness in reaching a predescribed target market. This is particularly true in media negotiations. A media negotiator's job is to get the most advertising time and space for the available budget. Unless given very tight buying parameters, a media negotiator will usually sacrifice the target richness of a media vehicle for one that is more cost efficient. This situation is particularly true in broadcast negotiations, where the choices are vast and the pressure to deliver a certain cost per thousand is high.

As an account planner, your role is not to negotiate a media buy; that's the media buyer's job. Rather, your role is to ensure that the members of the media negotiation team understand the target and will put a premium on reaching it. A savvy account planner can also help the media negotiation team by communicating with the client. The account planner can help the client better understand that it may not always be in their best interest to sacrifice the richness of a targeted media purchase by choosing a less expensive alternative.

Certainly for some brands, where the target market is a heavy consumer of media, cost efficiencies rule the day. But for brands that have a more discriminating target audience, looking for a medium that delivers the niche audience is more important than sheer bulk media impressions.

Regardless of the situation, the account planner can help guide both the client and media team to the right decision in the quest to balance efficiency versus effectiveness.

Role of Reach

A fundamental dimension of media planning is referred to as "reach." Reach can be viewed either vertically or horizontally. Vertical reach is the number of consumers you plan to reach on a weekly, monthly, or annual basis. Horizontal reach refers to the number of weeks you plan to advertise or the percentage of time you are covering. Figure 15.4 shows a sample of a reach matrix.

Media planners have much more sophisticated analysis than this simple matrix regarding the issue of reach. However, as the account planner, your role is to make sure that the media team is moving in the right direction and not to set specific reach and frequency goals. A discussion of reach using the matrix shown in Figure 15.4 is a place for the media team and client to start as they determine the focus of the campaign.

For example, if you were introducing a new sandwich from McDonald's featured at a "sharp" price point for a limited time, you would want to weigh vertical reach much more heavily than horizontal reach. You goal would be to tell as many people as possible about the new sandwich in the shortest amount of time.

Conversely, if you were continuing to remind consumers about Kraft's Macaroni and Cheese, then you might weigh horizontal reach more heavily than vertical reach. In this case, the goal would be to constantly remind consumers about the brand rather than to make sure that everyone knows about it in a short time.

The account planner can provide a framework for how the team should view the reach question.

Summary

Providing an integrated marketing communications plan is a detailed and complex process. Media professionals have extremely sophisticated analysis tools available to them that can help craft a plan. An integrated plan that involves public relations and digital professionals is the way to bring your overall strategy to life. The account planner can help these professionals shape their plans by providing more contexts about the consumer. The description of the target market plus a thorough briefing on how the brand is purchased can be a huge help to planning. Provid-

Figure 15.4   **Reach Matrix**

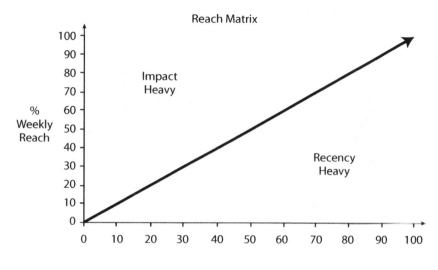

ing an understanding of the trade-offs between cost and target richness and the role that reach plays in the plan can also help to create the best plan for the client.

Review Questions

1. How do you define integrated marketing communications?
2. What are the different target audience needs for creative versus media versus public relations and digital areas of an advertising agency?
3. To what degree must brand positioning match up with media selection and vice versa?
4. What are the differences between quantitative and qualitative factors when selecting where to advertise? What are examples of each?

Discussion Questions

1. How does a product fit into a consumer's lifestyle? How does the lifestyle influence where to advertise?
2. How should advertising media be weighed in selection? How should it be weighed quantitatively? Qualitatively?
3. What kinds of products and services benefit most from vertical reach? Which need horizontal reach?

4. What role should media, digital, and public relations take in terms of IMC planning?

Additional Resources

Duncan, T. *Principles of Advertising and IMC.* New York: McGraw-Hill, 2004.

Kelley, T. *The Art of Innovation: Lessons in Creativity from IDEO, America's Leading Design Firm.* New York: Currency Books, 2001.

Kelley, T. *The Ten Faces of Innovation: IDEO's Strategies for Beating the Devil's Advocate and Driving Creativity throughout Your Organization.* New York: Doubleday, 2005.

Schultz, D., and H. Schultz. *IMC, the Next Generation: Five Steps for Delivering Value and Measuring Returns Using Marketing Communication.* New York: McGraw-Hill, 2003.

16

Measuring the Success of a Campaign

Any award-winning campaign must have a successful outcome; otherwise it won't win an award. But what makes it worthy of an award is a matter of interpretation. That is certainly where defining and measuring success comes into play. Whether you are a professional or in the student NSAC competition, defining success, putting together a program to be successful, and proving it by measuring the outcome is the formula for winning an award. The difference between a professional and a student competition is that the professionals actually measure campaigns that have been in the market while students are forecasting the impact of what their campaign may accomplish. However, in either case gauging success involves defining objectives and putting an evaluation or measurement plan into effect to understand if objectives have been achieved.

There are two overall areas that are measured: marketing objectives and advertising objectives. Figure 16.1 is an example of an NSAC award-winning plans book from the University of Virginia that shows how they would evaluate their proposed campaign.

The students outlined two overall components: business and brand objectives. In this case, the business objective was to increase the number of unique users to Yahoo! and to increase the time spent on the site. Expanding the number of products for those users was also a marketing objective. Increasing the differentiation of the brand from the competition was the brand objective.

From a communication standpoint, there are other objectives that link to the business and brand objectives. These involve the message, the creative, and the media or contact plan. The key questions or objectives to measure are as follows:

- Was the message compelling?
- Were the creative execution and strategy equally as compelling?
- Did the media selection or other activity run as planned?

171

Figure 16.1 **Yahoo! Campaign Evaluation**

Objective	Evaluation Technique
Drive registered Yahoo! users up 50 percent	• Track increase in registered users
	• Track concert kiosk usage
	• Measure ad recall
Increase "average time spent" on Yahoo! by 25 percent	• Use internal resources to measure "average time spent" on Yahoo! and on features.yahoo.com
Grow use of Yahoo! products by 1 on average	• Survey Seekers to determine the number of products used prior to the campaign
	• Compare to the number of products used by Seekers and Roadies in August 2006
Increase "differentiation" measure for Yahoo! by 10 percent	• Refer to Brand Asset Valuator
Enhance business-to-business opportunities with companies that seek to reach teens	• Measure increases in requests for Yahoo! Marketing services
	• Monitor the number of first-time teen advertisers

Each of these elements has specific measurement criteria. In this chapter we discuss aspects of campaign measurement from the specific communication measures to the overall business and brand metrics.

Lagging and Leading Indicators

Defining success is probably the most important aspect of developing an award-winning campaign. While defining success may seem like a simple exercise, you would be surprised by how many times a marketer and the agency disagree on the fundamentals of what success looks like.

The basic disagreement is between business goals and brand goals. Marketers are focused on generating business results. This may mean getting more consumers to buy the brand now. Or it might be to get consumers to buy more frequently. Whatever the consumer dynamic, the marketer is interested in growing his business. The agency is also interested in growing the client's business but from a different point of view. The agency focuses on building brand awareness or brand differentiation or changing a brand perception. While these measures are important, there are times when a company may believe that this is soft data, meaning it doesn't translate to bottom line sales.

The fallacy in that line of thinking is that generating sales and building the brand are two different tasks. They are not only interrelated, the brand metrics are actually a forecast of what the business metrics will be. A brand metric is a leading indicator and sales are a lagging indicator. If the brand is not known, or is misunderstood, this will ultimately lead to weak sales. In the meantime, the brand may be either discounting or offering a program to keep its current customers intact, which could mask what may become a long-term issue. So it is very important to understand the interplay between brand metrics and business metrics.

In the book *Brand Immortality* by Hamish Pringle and Peter Field, lagging and leading indicators are evaluated based on the history of IPA cases and applied to the product life cycle. The authors lead you through a metric checklist for the four stages of the product life cycle—introduction, growth, maturity, and decline—based on the correlation of these metrics to the ultimate success of the brand.

The following is a synopsis of the top leading and lagging indicators by product life cycle. This example demonstrates the types of metrics that should be evaluated depending upon the brand and the situation.

New Categories

1. Leading indicators   Brand awareness
Brand fame (the extent to which the brand gets talked about and is assumed to be an authoritative player in the new category)
Purchase intention
2. Lagging indicators   Trial levels
Penetration of usage
Market share

Growth Categories

1. Leading indicators   Brand fame
Perceived quality
Brand differentiation
2. Lagging indicators   Usage penetration
Trial levels
Market share

Mature Categories

1. Leading indicators   Brand fame
Perceived quality
Emotional brand differentiation
2. Lagging indicators   Price sensitivity
Market share
Usage penetration

Declining Categories

1. Leading indicators	Emotional brand differentiation
	Perceived quality
	Brand fame
2. Lagging indicators	Price sensitivity
	Market share
	Usage penetration

There are a number of lessons to be learned by studying the leading and lagging indicators of success that can help you evaluate what metrics are the most important.

- Beyond the initial stage of introducing a brand, simply being aware of a brand is not enough to make it successful.
- As the brand matures, the need for the brand to be famous (talked about or a part of the fabric of life) and to be clearly differentiated on a deep emotional level take on increasing importance.
- As the brand matures, the more important measure of success is the ability to raise price and steal share from other brands in the category.

Understanding what success is and how to measure it is the most crucial aspect of being an account planner. As you can see, there are likely to be very different takes on what success means. It is up to you to help guide all the stakeholders of the brand toward a common understanding of what success looks like and how you should measure it.

Awareness Attitude and Usage Studies

The place where most brands begin their measurement of success revolves around some form of awareness, attitude, and usage (AAU) study. These studies form the foundation for defining the problem that advertising must solve as well as providing a benchmark for how well the IMC program performs. These types of studies offer a good view of leading indicators. There is also a great deal of information available regarding brand sales and market share that are tracked as lagging indicators.

These studies are many times called tracking studies. The AAU revolves around understanding how consumers view the brand. Sales tracking involves understanding consumer behavior. The former represents perceptions of the brand while the latter represents facts about the brand. Ideally, a brand will work to correlate one with the other.

Let's discuss the sales analysis first. All companies track their sales to varying degrees of detail. A restaurant usually tracks the traffic count or number of people who come to the restaurant and the average amount of a check. Sales (S) in this case are calculated with a simple equation: traffic (T) multiplied by the average check (AC) ($S = T \times AC$). Variations of traffic count and average sale are the hallmarks of most retail tracking. It is pretty fundamental. Marketing's job is to get as many people as possible to visit the store and to ensure that they spend as much as possible once they are inside.

In packaged-goods marketing, there are syndicated research tools from A.C. Nielsen and Information Resources International that provide packaged-goods manufacturers with a rolling tally of unit sales. Because these systems are often linked to consumers through shopping or loyalty cards, there is a wealth of data available to the manufacturer regarding who is purchasing the brand and whether the brand was purchased using a coupon or an in-store special deal. Packaged-goods manufacturers use "penetration" and "buy rate" as their two primary behavioral measures. Penetration is how many different consumers purchase the brand. Buy rate refers to the frequency of purchase of the brand. Marketing's job is to increase the number of new users while maximizing frequency.

Business-to-business marketers also track customers and how much they spend. They may actually know the customer personally. While all companies and brands are interested in making money, business-to-business sales may evaluate each customer based on gross margin. A *gross margin* is how much each sale or customer contributes to the company's profits. Since business-to-business sales are usually based on a selective customer universe, it is paramount that the company evaluates each sale so that they are ensured a fair profit.

Sales tracking forms the basis for understanding how a brand is performing in the marketplace. Company managers may review it daily. As we have said, sales are a lagging indicator of success. That is why most brands develop AAU studies to measure what the consumer thinks of the brand. This involves questions about the level of awareness that the brand has in its target market. It also includes questions about how consumers view the brand versus alternatives in the category, and finally, there are questions about a consumer's intent to use the brand or switch from another brand to your brand. All of these measures form the basis for marketing and communications to both understand what the consumer issues are with the brand and how to measure a program based on fixing those issues.

There are two basic ways to conduct an AAU study. One method is to do a pre- and post-measure study. This type of study surveys consumers before a marketing communication program begins and then again at some designated point after the program has run. Most marketers conduct this type of research either quarterly, semiannually, or annually. These types of research studies are quantitative in nature. They usually consist of large enough sample sizes to be able to determine a statistically significant movement among the various aspects of the study. For example, if you survey a thousand consumers prior to a communications program and find that 20 percent are aware of your brand, and then conduct a post-wave survey with another thousand consumers that yields a 30 percent awareness level, movement is statistically significant (95 percent confidence level).

However, even with a large sample size, pre- and post-measure studies can be problematic. The timing of the study can significantly affect whether the results favor the communications impact. This is particularly true for a brand that is in a category that is purchased on a regular basis. Brands that are in the snack food or beverage category are purchased every week and may be prone to aggressive competitive activity. You may be conducting your post-measurement survey at the same time a competitor spends aggressively or offers a price promotion. So a onetime measure may be problematic. Depending on the results, the marketer and agency may quibble for weeks about the meaning of the study and the validity of the results.

That brings us to a second method for conducting this type of survey; the continuous tracking method. A continuous tracking method surveys consumers every week instead of sporadically. This way a marketer can see if there are things that may be impacting the program on an ongoing basis. This is why most makers of consumer-packaged goods use this methodology.

The combination of a continuous tracking methodology and a weekly sales tracking device creates a powerful diagnostic tool for determining how marketing and communications impact sales and brand perception. Figure 16.2 is an example of a continuous tracking scenario.

Regardless of the method, AAU studies are the staple of marketing and communication measurement. They are used before a campaign begins to understand the consumer problem at hand. They are used at the back end of the program to measure how effective it was. Student and professional campaigns make great use of this type of research in their campaigns. The difference between the two is that only the professionals implement both the pre- and post-wave research. Usually, student campaigns only implement pre-measure studies.

Isolating the Communication Effect

One key element of an award-winning professional campaign is the ability to isolate the communication effect on the outcome. This is not an easy task.

Figure 16.2 **Key Measurement Summary**

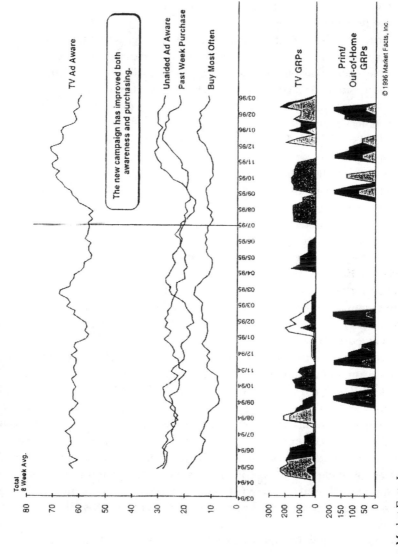

Source: Market Facts Inc.

Many people believe that it is not possible to measure the effect of communication. Even if you can measure it, it is difficult to say if communication is the real reason for success. For example, if you ran a communications program for a client where the competition suddenly raised its price, how can you determine if the incremental sales your client gained came from the communications or from the competitive action? Perhaps it is a combination of the two, but in what proportion?

To answer these questions, marketers and their agency partners are turning to sophisticated statistical models. Driven largely by the consumer packaged-goods industry, marketing mix modeling is the analysis that uses econometric modeling techniques to understand what factors contribute the most to sales.

These marketing heuristics are available now more than ever because of the endless supply of grocery scanner data. This allows marketers to analyze granular (tiny) bits of information. Using two or more years of information with hundreds of observations, an econometric model can be developed that helps explain how the components of communications contribute to sales. All of these methods use sophisticated multivariate statistical analysis with senior research personnel at the helm.

This type of analysis has taken hold in advertising media planning departments. In our book *Advertising Media Planning: A Brand Management Approach,* we provide an example of a marketing mix exercise for a fictitious product, Bob's Baked Beans. Figure 16.3 shows the analysis. The outcome is that for every dollar that Bob's Baked Beans spends on advertising, the brand generates $1.50. This is a much higher return than other marketing elements in the mix. So, it would appear that Bob's Baked Beans is highly sensitive to advertising.

The majority of firms that market consumer packaged goods conduct some form of marketing mix modeling. Advertising media departments are also involved in developing these models as they relate to communications planning. The purpose of the models not only isolates the communications variables but ultimately it can be used as a forecasting tool for the brand.

As an account planner, your role in this process is not to get out your statistics book and figure out the dynamics of these variables. You should leave this to the statistical professionals. However, your mission is to ensure that the tool is used properly. One shortcoming of marketing mix modeling is that it focuses on the past. Just because you can understand the past doesn't mean that you can explain the future.

But the rise of marketing mix modeling has shown that communications can lead to significant business results. In fact, an IPA case won't pass muster if it doesn't isolate the impact of communications on the specific business objective.

Figure 16.3 **Bob's Baked Beans**

Marketing Mix Model: Bob's Beans	
Item	**Incremental Profit Per $1.00 Spent**
Media Advertising	$1.50
FSI Coupons	$1.00
Trade Promotions	$0.85

Communication Measurement

A communication campaign or execution within a campaign must do the following three things to be successful.

1. The message must be compelling enough to motivate the target to take the action you want them to take.
2. It must be noticed by the target market and remembered.
3. Your target market must know who is speaking to them. The brand must be appropriately linked to the communication effort. This is called brand linkage.

The message that you are communicating is the central aspect of any campaign. One method to ensure that the right message is conveyed is through research called concept testing. Concept testing can be done a number of ways. At its heart is a test of the value proposition of the brand. If the value proposition is simple, the concept testing may be done just with brand statements that are simple ways of translating a brand position. For example, Crisco oil could be positioned as:

- Trusted by generations of women
- Most popular brand of cooking oil
- Makes your dishes come out right every time
- Your family will love you for it
- It makes cooking a breeze

These statements could be shown to consumers for feedback. Some marketers use graphics along with key ideas to evoke a greater set of emotions from respondents. Testing messages is a crucial first step in any campaign. As the latter shows, Crisco could be tapping into themes ranging from heritage to convenience to a family hero.

Not every brand has a straightforward value proposition. Take Nike, for example. The advertising for Nike is a part of the brand. The benefit is that Nike will transform you to be an athletic star. But you wouldn't get very far testing a value proposition like that. That is why many brands use other testing methods to get after what to say and how to say it.

Rational Versus Emotional Message

A good way to begin a dialogue on how best to test message and communication execution is to look at the type of message you will be communicating. For example, communicating that you have a one-day sale is a whole lot different than communicating that if you drink a certain beer you will get the girl of your dreams. The more rational the communication, the easier it is to test. The more emotional the communication, it is difficult to test if it hits the desired emotional chord or if it motivates the consumer to take action.

One way to begin the process is by evaluating your message on a simple message emphasis measure. Figure 16.4 demonstrates the method. Here you can evaluate your message along the scale from rational to emotional. By working with the client on this simple exercise, you can come to grips with what type of communication you are working with and what might be the appropriate method to measure its success.

To the far left are the most rational messages. These can be things like a one-day sale or a limited-time offer such as Subway's $5 foot-long sandwich. The rational side doesn't have to be sales messages. It can also be informational announcements. It might be announcing a new company or a new store opening. It is high on information.

The next stage in the process is the functional benefit. It can be that Hershey's candy bars are now 50 percent larger or that Tide has a new cleaning agent. It might be that E*TRADE is now bundling insurance with mutual funds. Functional benefits have long been the mainstay of the advertising industry. If you have a unique feature, you should ride it before the competition matches it.

Before we move to the emotional side of the scale, we need to clarify that just because your key message is rational doesn't mean that your communication needs to be. You can make an emotional appeal with a one-day sale or a new $1 item on a fast-food value menu. The purpose of the grid is not to suggest that everything on the left side is blasé and everything on the right is not. Some of the best communication comes from delivering a rational message in a unique manner. The purpose of the grid is to understand the core message and how to test it.

As we move from functional benefit to emotional benefit, it is just like

Figure 16.4   **Message Emphasis Measure**

Message Emphasis									
Rational									Emotional
1	2	3	4	5	6	7	8	9	10
Sales Messages			Functional Benefits			Emotional Benefits as result of Functional			Pure Emotional Benefit

moving up the benefit ladder. In the case of Hershey's increasing its portions by 50 percent, that could lead to a greater chocolate indulgence. That is marketing the effect of the effect. As we have said before, the emotional side of the scale is how the message makes the consumer feel.

The final stage is a pure emotional message. Most cosmetics, liquor, and entertainment brands are based on satisfying an emotional benefit. Instead of a one-day sale of the product or service, you would have to look at different methods of measuring the impact of the message over time. Let's look at the various methods used to evaluate communication.

Qualitative Testing

The most commonly used method for testing messages and creative execution is through qualitative research. Qualitative research offers spontaneous, rich, and undirected feedback. That is exactly what you are looking for when evaluating how a message or commercial hits you.

Let's face it, you are just not likely to fill out a questionnaire saying that a commercial moved you or made you laugh. But observing how consumers actually react to communication is a good barometer of how it will work in the marketplace.

Many advertisers use focus groups as the standard bearer for testing creative concepts and messages. Focus groups consist of a trained moderator working with eight to twelve consumers of similar characteristics. The consumers are recruited to a focus group facility where the advertiser and agency can view the participants through a one-way mirror.

The popularity of focus groups is that within an hour or two the advertiser and agency can see reactions from consumers. Focus groups usually have some form of interplay between respondents. There are pros and cons to this interaction. Sometimes it can lead to a rich insight. Other times, a dominant personality can sway other members.

The artificial nature of focus groups along with the unpredictable group dynamics has led many marketers to look elsewhere for deep insights.

Perhaps the best insights come from one-on-one interviews where the moderator and the consumer can engage in a deeper conversation about their emotions. This is not possible in a group setting. One of the leaders in this area is Gerald Zaltman who has pioneered a one–on–one metaphorical research method called ZMET interviews, which was previously discussed in Chapter 6. In this process, consumers bring in pictures and other items that are metaphors for the brand. They can be shown advertising or other communication to get at their deeper feelings for the brand.

The upside of qualitative research is that you can get a feel for the kind of emotional response the communication will deliver. You can see individuals' "gut" reaction and determine if you are connecting with them on an emotional level.

The downside of qualitative research is that it is based on feelings and is therefore not quantifiable. When a CEO is investing millions of dollars into a marketing program, there is a reluctance to do so based on a sample of ten or twelve people. From a communication perspective, while you may have a feel for what works, there is no guarantee that the message will motivate consumers to act the way you hope they will act.

Brain Science in Qualitative Research

A new wave in research employs technology that is used in psycho-physiological studies of the brain. These companies offer a marketer the best of both worlds. They can measure the emotional reaction to communication and get a statistically significant result.

One company in this area is Sensory Logic. They use a combination of facial coding, galvanic skin response, and a written diagnostic to measure emotional reaction to various stimuli. By tracking the facial expression of the respondent, Sensory Logic can provide a second-by-second emotional analysis of a consumer's reaction to a television commercial. By comparing this with the written diagnostic on traditional measures such as main message recall and likeability, a marketer can determine if the key message was registered as well as the emotional nature of it.

Another company that symbolizes this new era of research is Neurofocus. This company uses MRI technology to understand the brain activity level of various stimuli. Similar to Sensory Logic, Neurofocus can assess second-by-second emotional reaction to a television commercial by analyzing the brain activity in a respondent.

These two companies are emblematic of the new methods and technologies that marketers can use to get at the emotional connection between their brand and the consumer.

Copytesting

Copytesting is a term covering a broad range of advertising research techniques. For some companies and agencies, copytesting is pre-creative, meaning that it is used before the final form of the actual advertising. For others, copytesting is used to show more than concepts but less than finished creative to determine how to tweak a message. Others use copytesting to measure finished advertisements to determine how they stack up against the competition.

There is a dizzying array of companies and methodologies that provide copytesting services. Each has its pros and cons. As the account planner, it is up to you to help guide this process. Before embarking on any copytesting, there are some fundamental questions to resolve.

1. What do we expect the advertising to do?
2. What is our view of how advertising works?
3. What will we do with the research outcome?

Once these issues are agreed upon, then you can decide what the most appropriate method is to test it. Let's take a look at each of these questions and how it could impact your methodological selection.

The first question is a pretty basic issue. What do we expect the advertising to do? Do we expect it to make an immediate sale or do we want it to change an attitude? Do we want to switch a competitive user to our brand? These are all valid outcomes. Each outcome might lend itself to a different measure of success. One focuses on purchase intent, another on attitudinal change, and the last on competitive differentiation.

The second question regarding how advertising works is not a trick question. Many research companies utilize specific methods based on their view of how advertising works. If you believe in their method then you should consider it. If not, you should pass.

The third question addresses the results of research. Is the outcome designed to see how the creative may perform in the market? Or is it designed to provide feedback to the creative group to improve the product? Each of these outcomes may necessitate a different methodology.

The final question is, what happens if the creative tests poorly? Do you scrap the campaign and start over? Or is there something that you should change to make the campaign effective? All of these issues should be discussed beforehand rather than waiting until it may be too late to impact the process.

Once you agree on the answers to these questions, you are off and running. Now it is time to pick the most appropriate method for the task at hand.

Copytesting Methods

There are a number of companies that do copytesting. Many have specialized methods to do so. Many have quantitative diagnostics based on the large number of commercials that they have tested and/or in market validation of their method. This is why many marketers use copytesting for creative executions. They can gain confidence about how the commercial performs compared to normative values and can gain information that forecasts how the creative will perform in the marketplace.

Before we get into the different methods of copytesting, it is important to understand the dividing line for most researchers about how advertising works. The research community is divided into two camps. The first camp is recall based and the second camp is persuasion based.

Since the early days of television, the first widely used pretesting measure for this medium was based on the research company Burke. Burke had developed a method called day-after recall score. The measure was based on how many consumers could remember an ad the day after they saw it on television. Day-after recall was a memory test; it measured how memorable the advertising was.

Recall is based on the simple principle that advertising that is remembered works better than advertising that isn't. However, during the 1970s Procter & Gamble, the world's largest packaged-goods company, concluded that recall of commercials did not necessarily correlate with sales. Although subsequent research has shown that recall does indeed correlate with sales, this Procter & Gamble study rocked the research world.

In the 1970s copytesting research shifted gears from recall to persuasion, the actual change in preference on the part of the customer. This view of communication is that the message should be able to convert into short-term sales. This research goes on to indicate that this conversion could be predicted within the market. The degree of conversion is measured by taking a split sample (control and test group with one half shown the commercial and the other not) and measuring the difference between the purchase intent between the two groups.

Many large packaged-goods companies like Procter & Gamble use this approach and build large databases of research on brand commercials so that they can view them comparatively and historically. Some use these databases to forecast how much incremental sales lift they get from various types of appeals.

One of the leading research companies in this area is Ipsos ASI. Ipsos ASI has developed a copy-effect score. This score combines recall and persuasion into a single diagnostic that indicates the net communication effect.

Their copy-effect index (CEI) score is then used as a barometer of success for creative execution. Figure 16.5 is an example of how the CEI correlates with sales for a selective packaged-goods category.

As you can see from this example, the CEI serves as a strong indicator of a commercial's short-term or incremental volume effects on a brand. Those commercials having a CEI of less than a 70 do not generate much incremental volume. Those with a CEI of greater than 130 generate a lot of incremental volume. For many marketers, this type of measurement is used as a benchmark for commercials that are aired and those that don't see the light of day. Since the focus is on short-term volume rather than longer-term attributes, it is very appealing to brand managers or chief marketing officers who are under pressure to impact sales immediately.

Meanwhile, others continue to argue that how much a person likes a commercial is the key to its success. Likeability was empirically confirmed as a predictor of success by an Advertising Research Foundation project and paper in 1991. Many agencies and marketers still look to likeability as the key measure for communication execution success.

Regardless of the method used, most copytesting methods that use quantitative analysis rely on the use of normative data. Normative data is comparing your communication to a database of historical advertisements. So your advertisement is graded or compared to others based on the diagnostics of "attention getting" and "persuasion." This normative database could be very broad such as all food companies or it could be very specific such as canned pasta advertisers. While normative data can be very appealing for advertisers, it can also be misleading. No two advertising commercials are designed for the same purpose or for identical target markets. It is important to keep this in mind when analyzing your commercial in relationship to past efforts.

Even though communication research has given us much richer diagnostics than in the past, judgments still need to be made. One cannot totally abdicate responsibility for communication by merely seeing whether it hits a certain copytesting metric. Research can certainly improve communication and also reduce the risks associated with it. While it can help you make a decision, there is no substitute for common sense and experience.

As the account planner, you are at the center of this process. On one side, you want to make sure that the creative team doesn't have the soul taken out of its effort by being a slave to research. On the other hand, you must help reassure the client who is ultimately responsible for the advertising that it will meet its objectives. This is not always an easy task, but by working through the issues, you can make the best communication to accomplish the goal.

Figure 16.5   Incremental Volume

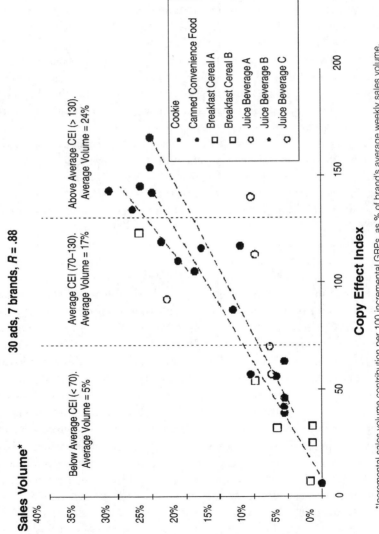

Sales Volume*

30 ads, 7 brands, R = .88

Below Average CEI (< 70).
Average Volume = 5%

Average CEI (70–130).
Average Volume = 17%

Above Average CEI (> 130).
Average Volume = 24%

Copy Effect Index

Cookie
Canned Convenience Food
Breakfast Cereal A
Breakfast Cereal B
Juice Beverage A
Juice Beverage B
Juice Beverage C

*Incremental sales volume contribution per 100 incremental GRPs, as % of brand's average weekly sales volume.

Figure 16.6   **Typical Communication Effect Research**

Type of communication effect	→	Typical research
• Sales	→	Company database and records
• Consumer buying behavior	→	Retail scanning data and/or customer research
• Consumer purchase intent	→	Primary quantitative research
• Attitudes toward brand	→	Primary quantitative tracking research
• Awareness of the brand	→	Primary quantitative tracking research
• Attitudes of brand	→	Primary quantitative tracking research for market changes and qualitative research for executions
• Recall of communication	→	Primary quantitative tracking research
	→	Copytesting
• Exposure to communication	→	Syndicated media research
	→	AAU

Advertising Effects and Research Methods

We have discussed a wide range of issues and success criteria for an award-winning campaign. From a communication perspective, there are some fairly standard measures even though there are a myriad of methodologies used to arrive at them. Figure 16.6 offers a recap of the communication effect and the typical research methodology employed to understand it.

As you move through the course of measuring a communication campaign, it is important to keep in mind that there are short-term and long-term effects of any effort. The short-term effects are captured in purchase behavior information. The long-term aspects are captured in attitudinal studies. The diagnostics of message, creative execution, and media pressure can be captured through a combination of the research we have discussed.

In conclusion, it is important to remember that communication works in many different ways. To build an award-winning campaign, you must help your client initially define success from a business and brand perspective. Then you should link the role that communications will play in that success. Ultimately, the success of the agency will be based on the success of the advertiser. No matter how the metrics are defined, an award-winning campaign cannot be done without trust between the agency and advertiser.

Review Questions

1. What is brand equity? How would you measure it?
2. What is the difference between awareness, attitude, and usage? How are they interrelated?

3. What is a tracking study? What are the different methods for conducting it?
4. What is the difference between measuring rational versus emotional factors in communication?
5. What is copytesting? What are the key measures in a copy test?

Discussion Questions

1. How can awareness, attitude, and usage be matched up to create an analysis of success?
2. How can building brand equity be tracked to match with advertising success?
3. What is the real measure of communication success?
4. Should copytesting be used to measure communication?

Additional Resources

Hill, D. *Emotiononics: Leveraging Emotions for Business Success*. Philadelphia: Adams, 2007.
Pringle, H., and P. Field. *Brand Immortality: How Brands Can Live Long and Prosper.* London: Institute of Practitioners in Advertising, 2009.
Tellis, G. *Effective Advertising: Understanding When, How, and Why Advertising Works*. Newbury Park, CA: Sage, 2003.

17

Business-to-Business Case Study

Recon Software

Recon Software is the brainchild of two graduate students at the University of California at Berkeley. Their initial work involved optimizing production systems through the use of neural network software. However, they discovered that they could use this same tool to build an ever-upgraded firewall providing a defense against computer viruses. They quickly patented the neural network software and named it Recon. The name is short for *reconnaissance*.

Recon software gained strength as the product gained server mass. Because it was a constantly learning program, the more servers and defense to which it had access, the greater the ability of the software to learn what viruses were possible. This information fed into the software's ability to upgrade itself continually and to block not only existing viruses but to predict and adapt to future viruses as well.

The student's professor introduced the two students to a Silicon Valley venture capital firm that provided the seed money to develop the software and take it to market. The two students formed their company and promptly enlisted the help of an advertising agency to market the product. The venture capital company had given Recon only a six-month timeframe in which to launch their product before the bank "pulled" its funding. Making the right decision in terms of positioning and marketing was crucial for the young entrepreneurs.

Software Marketplace

The software marketplace was huge (see Figure 17.1 and Table 17.1). The defense segment into which the two students stumbled was a nearly $10 billion worldwide market. The major players in this market were IBM, which dominated computer mainframe protection, other aggressive companies,

Figure 17.1 **Worldwide Total Network Security Revenue**

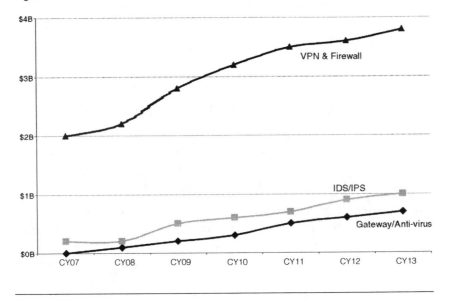

Table 17.1

Worldwide Security Software Market Forecast by Channels: 2005 to 2008
($ millions)

		Year			Compound annual growth (%)
Channels	2005	2006	2007	2008	(2005–8)
Direct	5,357	6,065	6,082	7,510	11.9
Multi-tier Distribution	2,513	2,844	3,189	3,520	11.9
OEM	1,047	1,166	1,286	1,395	10.1
Single-tier resale	3,033	3,618	4,269	4,950	17.7
Total	11,950	13,694	15,546	17,375	13.3

such as Oracle, Computer Associates, and niche companies, such as BMC Software. All of these companies had products in the defense arena, with the latter three more server-based and IBM more mainframe-based.

The companies that could benefit most from Recon's software were very large companies with complex computer systems. The venture capital team helped the students identify the target markets and groups. The more complex systems included pulp and paper mills, auto manufacturing plants, oil refineries, electric and gas utilities, and the local, state, and national government, as shown in Table 17.2.

Table 17.2

Systems Software Market

Category	Headquarter companies (number)	Total software revenue ($ billions)
Pulp and paper mills	10	5.2
Auto manufacturing	20	7.9
Oil refineries	30	7.4
Gas/electric utilities	300	12.3
Government (city, state, and federal)	7,000	45.2
Total	7,495	78.0

All of these companies would benefit from Recon's software because they could link all their plants to the same defense software programs that could learn from one another to maximize their virus protection. However, the systems of all of these companies were well established and the students wondered whether the companies would be likely to try something new. The "going-in" or entry cost for Recon was not inexpensive. The cost was $500,000 to set up the system plus a minimum monthly fee of $10,000 that escalated depending upon the server volume of the company.

On the other hand, if a plant had a business interruption of one day it could cost the company well over $1 million. In other cases, an outage of any type would have dire consequences (see Table 17.3).

Table 17.3

Cost of Business Interruption

Category	Dollars per day per single plant ($ millions)
Pulp and paper mills	0.7
Auto manufacturing	1.2
Oil refineries	3
Gas/electric utilities	2.2
Government (city, state, and federal)	1.5

To complicate things more, the students learned that there were multiple layers to selling this type of business product. There were IT (information technology) managers who had to be consulted on any software purchase. IT was responsible for maintaining and installing the product. There were operations managers who depended on the software to help them with their jobs. There were financial managers who reviewed all purchases and a senior

Figure 17.2   **Risk-Reward Matrix**

manager who had to give the final blessing. This was nothing compared to selling to the government. The pair learned that they must first apply to be a government contractor and then go through a bidding process before being considered.

To help the students get through this process, a veteran software marketer developed a risk/reward matrix to help them understand the decision process and how each position would react to the new software (see Figure 17.2). He also hired some young and aggressive salespeople who could go anywhere to make the sale.

The students were very excited about their software and thought Recon was a "cool" name. Their first thought was to position this as a hip new product. Yet they were concerned that if they appeared to be too irreverent they would not be taken seriously.

This information constituted the briefing that the account planner was given for Recon software. The account planner knew it was largely up to him to help bring some clarity to this situation for Recon. The students were inexperienced in marketing and the venture team had provided working capital but not much else. This project would involve market analysis, positioning, and ultimately some sort of marketing communications program to sell the software. And time was of the essence; the salespeople were clamoring for sales materials and marketing support.

The account planner quickly looked for any information he could find on his audience. He came across a few articles that shed some light on buyer

Table 17.4

Target Profile

Occupation	Typical demographics	Occupational mind-set
IT	Male, age 35–45, college grad	Looks for latest technology to make a difference
Operations	Male, age 35–45, some college	Looks to keep things running smoothly and quickly
Finance	Male, age 45–60, MBA	Looks to control costs and save money where possible
Management	Male, age 45–65, college/MBA	Looking for competitive edge

behavior for large purchases by companies. Table 17.4 associated a "face" with the various target markets of the major companies to which they would be selling.

There was not a lot of time to lose. The account planner had only a few weeks to put a plan together for Recon.

The Assignment

1. Determine the best segment and target(s) to gain the quickest stronghold into the market.
2. Determine the best positioning for that segment.
3. Determine the best marketing and advertising strategy to promote Recon to that segment.
4. Translate the strategy into a creative brief.
5. Determine what research is needed for the brand while doing the initial plan.
6. Provide a point of view on positioning Recon in short-term versus long-term positioning of the brand.

18

Packaged-Goods Case Study

Chiffon Margarine

Pinnacle Foods is an aggregator of venerable old brands that are in need of restaging. One of the recently acquired brands in its stable of products was Chiffon margarine. Chiffon had great success in the 1970s and 1980s as one of the brand leaders when butter surrendered to margarine as the spread of choice. During this time, Chiffon had some award-winning advertising with "Mother Nature" as the spokesperson for the brand. In the television commercial executions, "Mother Nature" would proclaim Chiffon was so fresh and natural that "It isn't nice to fool Mother Nature."

Since the 1980s, the Chiffon brand has been bought and sold more than once. It became largely a trade-supported brand with no advertising or marketing for ten years. However, the new brand manager on Chiffon at Pinnacle Foods felt that the brand had some "upside" potential. The firm had come up with a break-through way of enhancing the brand with natural flavors. Based on significant product testing, Pinnacle was ready to "roll out" sweetened and unsweetened versions of the margarine as well as margarine with cinnamon flavoring. The brand manager felt that he could do with margarine what had been done in other food categories such as mustard, ketchup, and other condiments, creating some excitement and new usage opportunities. He also felt that he could take some market share away from the cooking sprays and oils that now had flavorings but were inconsistent in their usage.

As he saw the product benefits, there was a natural flavoring of foods that he felt was very appealing. A homemaker could basically enhance any meal without changing the way it was prepared. In today's fast-paced world, he felt that benefit would be very appealing. The flavorings were also all-natural, which kept with the natural tradition of the brand, which he also felt was a big plus. The margarine fared very well in taste tests,

Table 18.1

Chiffon Case: Margarine Category

Total category sales: $861.5 million

Brand	Share (%)	Advertising used
Private label	23.5	None
I Can't Believe It's Not Butter	12.7	TV, Print
Shedd's County Crock	11.6	TV, Print
Blue Bonnet	10.9	FSI
Parkay	8.5	TV, FSI
Imperial	8.5	None
Land O'Lakes	5.5	TV
Fleishmann's	4.0	Print
Chiffon	2.0	None
Other brands (local/regional)	12.8	—
Total	100.0	

with consumers saying the cinnamon flavor really enhanced their foods. Others talked about how they liked the sweeter margarine. Consumers said that this characteristic made up for not using sugar or other sweeteners in their cooking. This final focus group got the brand manager thinking there might even be a nutritional angle that he might be able to exploit in the brand's advertising.

The margarine category represents $861.5 million of revenue with a host of brands competing for market share. There was quite a bit of competition for this market, with the majority of brands spending many dollars on marketing. The medium of choice for the category was television. Many of the brands also used women's magazines as an advertising medium and many also used coupons distributed in freestanding inserts.

Table 18.1 summarizes the competition and the market share.

As the brand manager reviewed the category, he was concerned about the large private-label percentage of sales. This signaled to him that the category had deteriorated into a general commodity. He wanted the new flavors of Chiffon to command a premium price, but he feared the category might not be able to support a more premium-priced entry. He was also concerned Chiffon had become a "price brand," competing and selling on low price, because it had quit advertising long ago. It would be a tough road to command a premium price for Chiffon given its low market share and history of not supporting the brand with marketing support.

The advertising agency had just completed an assignment on defining the demographics of the category (see Table 18.2). The category consumer was a housewife, 25 to 54 years of age, who was married and had two

Table 18.2

Margarine Category: Frequent User

Demographics	Users (%)	Index
Females	75	150
18–24	9	80
25–34	17	100
35–44	21	105
45–54	22	110
55–64	16	108
65+	15	90
Grad college +	20	80
Any college	24	60
HS grad	36	107
HS not grad	20	133
Employed fulltime	60	115
Married	65	112
1 child in home	18	105
2–3 in home	22	125
4+ in home	15	132

children. The frequent buyers of margarine also were not highly educated, which concerned the brand manager as he considered how he might position the product. A debate raged in the company about whom he should target. Should it be the current category user, or should he stake out some ground with consumers who were very much in tune with the brand regardless of how much margarine they used?

To shed more light on the margarine consumer, the advertising agency also profiled the margarine consumer's buying lifestyles. Table 18.3 shows the key buying lifestyles that the agency found of interest.

After reviewing the buying lifestyles, the brand manager became very concerned about what to think. He saw that the consumers indicated that they would not pay for quality and they made impulsive purchases. Could he get them to take a chance and try his brand?

The advertising agency also delved into some consumer-trend information on food trends and found that there were a few key areas that were very applicable to this situation.

As the brand manager reviewed the values shown in Table 18.4, he was becoming even more confused. He saw the trends were in his favor, but on which one should he focus?

Table 18.3

Chiffon Case: Margarine Consumer Buying Styles

Attitude	Index
Enjoy spending time with my family	130
I like to do unconventional things	95
Important to be attractive	120
Worth paying extra for quality	85
Decide what I want before shopping	75
I am easily swayed by others	110
I am the first to try new things	100
I buy items on impulse	140

Source: Simmons Market Research Bureau.

Table 18.4

Top Ten Consumer Food Values

Value	Referred (%)
Deliciousness	41
Convenience	21
Wellness	20
Experience	14
Fun	13
Quality	12
Simplicity	12
Balance	12
Authenticity	11
Control	10

Source: Iconoculture. Reprinted with permission.

The agency also came across some research discussing the body types of various consumers (see Table 18.5). The researchers looked at the frequent margarine buyer but also looked at consumers who liked spicy foods as an indicator of consumers who might try new items. The results of the study showed there were marked differences between the two groups.

Now the brand manager's head was spinning. He called a brand summit meeting with the advertising agency team to discuss all the research and the brand. He said that the agency needed to sift through the data and give him a recommendation on how to proceed with supporting the brand. The agency president turned to the account planner and gave him the following assignment.

Table 18.5

Chiffon Case: Waist Brand Study

Type	Frequent margarine user	Spicy food eater
Underweight	62	110
Normal	91	120
Overweight	115	105
Obesity	135	75

Source: Simmons Market Research Bureau.

Assignment

1. Determine the appropriate brand position for Chiffon and, based on that positioning, develop a creative brief for the agency.
2. Before determining the positioning we need to develop a recommendation on the best target market to tackle with this brand.
3. Because Chiffon had some advertising that was quite good in its day, perhaps we should review it and consider writing a story about it and the brand.
4. While we don't have much media information to go on, we should get the media team prepared to help launch this brand.

19

Retail Case Study

Kmart and Sears

It is not every day an account planner sits in the office of the chairman of one of the largest retail holding companies in the world, but there you sit by the desk of the man who just orchestrated the merger of Kmart and Sears to form Sears Holding Company.

He has asked for you to come to his office because he has an enormous task ahead of him. Now that he owns both Kmart and Sears, what should he do with them? Should he combine them into one brand? And if so, which brand should he choose? Or should he keep them as two separate brands and try to outflank Walmart and Target, the key competitors in the discount retailing arena?

As the chairman mulled over these decisions, he called you into his office because he wanted to get a consumer perspective on this decision without any emotional bias. Obviously, the marketing directors of each company, Sears and Kmart, have reasons for wanting to maintain control over their marketing decisions. Because he knows you are with the advertising agency that is going to support the brand regardless of its outcome, he has called you into the office to gain your perspective on this move.

He first explains why he merged Kmart with Sears. He felt that size and scope were the only way to compete in the retailing world dominated by Walmart. Table 19.1 demonstrates that very point. However, even the combined Kmart and Sears entity was only a quarter the size of Walmart.

The chairman goes on to say he feels that there would be operational efficiencies in buying merchandise and having central warehouses for both chains. He sees there is potential to sell some of Sears' brand merchandise, particularly Kenmore appliances and Craftsman tools, in Kmart. Plus, he sees potential to sell some of Kmart's fashion brands, such as Martha Stewart, Route 66, and Jaclyn Smith, in Sears stores. But he feels that both Sears and Kmart are not great overall brands. To him, Sears seems dated while Kmart is still known as the "blue light special" place.

Table 19.1

Top Retail Sales Leaders

Company	Revenue
Walmart	174.2
Sears	23.2
Target	41.3
Kmart	23.0
Federated Stores	17.7
May Co.	15.0
	14.0

Source: Retail Business Market Research Handbook.

Table 19.2

Key Brands Owned by Each Retailer

Sears	Kmart
Lands End	Martha Stewart
Craftsmen Tools	Jaclyn Smith
Kenmore Appliances	Joe Boxer
Whirlpool	Route 66
Frigidaire	Sesame Street

Although both Sears and Kmart have fashion brands (see Table 19.2), neither has made much progress in cracking the discount fashion business, which Target now dominates. Even Walmart is having a tough time catching Target in this important facet of merchandising. It is one of the key areas that consistently brings customers to the store. This concerns the chairman considerably. He needs to make the right move with the brands and he needs to build a retailer of the future. The Chairman asks you to come back in two weeks with a recommendation on how you see the business from a consumer perspective and how this view might determine the marketing and advertising approach for the company.

The next day, the president of the advertising agency meets with you and your planning team to discuss the situation. During the course of discussion, the planning team has begun to assemble various pieces of research that might be helpful in figuring out the two brands.

One interesting piece of research that the planning team has come across is a cross-shopping matrix showing the percent of shoppers who shop at various retailers and a loyalty factor for each (see Table 19.3).

The team also had asked the media team to develop a demographic profile of Kmart and Sears consumers. Table 19.4 shows the profile of each customer base.

Table 19.3

Cross Shopping of Consumers Regarding Mass Merchandising

Company	Sears consumers who shop at (%)	Kmart consumers who shop at (%)	Consumers who shop predominantly at (%)
Sears	100	35	20
Kmart	20	100	10
Walmart	85	90	50
Target	60	70	40

Table 19.4

Demographic Profile of Sears and Kmart Shopper

Demographic	Sears %	Sears Index	Kmart %	Kmart Index
Male	45	94	36	75
Female	55	106	64	123
18–24	4	34	9	79
25–34	13	78	17	99
35–44	18	04	21	105
45–54	26	131	22	110
55–64	19	128	16	108
65+	20	115	15	90
Median HHI	$63,000		$52,000	
Married	74	127	58	90
Not Married	36	85	42	110
White	84	108	77	99
African American	9	90	12	120
Hispanic	7	65	11	135

Source: Mediamark Research, Inc. Reprinted with permission.

The team has also identified consumer buying lifestyles that the two brands have in common and those that are unique to each (see Table 19.5).

After reviewing this information, the president asks whether you feel that you could make an agency recommendation from it. He is concerned it isn't enough information from which to draw the proper insights that could ultimately lead to making important decisions. The president of the agency says that he would be willing to fund primary research to understand the situation better, but with time so short, what could be done that would be meaningful?

Table 19.5

Buying Styles of Mass Merchandiser Consumers

Buying Statement	Kmart	Sears	Target	Walmart
I am an impulsive shopper	116	95	125	105
I am willing to pay more for quality	105	125	120	90
I enjoy owning good things	130	110	140	105
I am always looking for new ideas	115	90	135	115
I like a simple life	80	140	85	110
I am good at fixing things	100	150	95	120
I decide what I want before shopping	90	125	80	120
I am optimistic	115	105	120	105
I find that I am swayed easily by others	120	90	130	105
I try not to worry about the future	115	105	120	105

Source: Simmons Market Research Bureau.

While the assignment seems clear, the president of the agency decides to write up the assignment just to ensure everyone has the proper focus on what to accomplish.

Assignment

1. Develop a SWOT analysis to understand better where the opportunities are for the two brands.
2. Develop a positioning exercise for each brand and determine where you might position each separately.
3. From this positioning exercise, determine whether one brand is clearly superior to another.
4. Develop a creative brief for the brand or brands that survive the positioning exercise.
5. Develop a research plan to help map out a process for success and how to track progress toward it.

Index

About the Authors

Larry D. Kelley is an educator, author, and advertising professional. His areas of specialization include advertising account planning as well as integrated marketing communications planning.

Mr. Kelley is a Professor of Advertising at the University of Houston Valenti School of Communication where he heads the advertising program. He teaches advertising account planning and media planning and is the faculty advisor for the AAF-NSAC campaigns team.

Mr. Kelley is the author or coauthor of six textbooks on advertising as well as a popular culture book. *Advertising Media Planning: A Brand Management Approach* and its corresponding *Workbook and Sourcebook, Advertising Account Planning: A Practical Approach,* and *Advertising and Public Relations Research* have been widely adopted at the university level.

Mr. Kelley is also a Partner at FKM in Houston, Texas, the sixtieth largest advertising firm in the United States, where he is Chief Planning Officer. Prior to joining FKM in 1990, Mr. Kelley served in senior media and research positions with BBD&O, Bozell & Jacobs, and the Bloom Agency.

Mr. Kelley has worked with a wide variety of clients and categories for both domestic and international campaigns. Some of the clients that he has worked with include American Airlines, Coca-Cola Foods, ConAgra Foods, Conoco/Phillips, Dell, Georgia-Pacific, Kroger, Waste Management, and Yum brands. He has been awarded four EFFIES for advertising effectiveness as well as numerous ADDY awards.

Mr. Kelley holds a bachelor of science in journalism from the University of Kansas and a master's degree in advertising from the University of Texas at Austin.

Dr. Donald W. Jugenheimer is an author, researcher, consultant, and educator. His specialties are interpersonal and mass communications with emphasis on personal communication, advertising and media management, media economics, and advertising media.

As a consultant, Dr. Jugenheimer has worked with such firms as American Airlines, IBM, Century 21 real estate, Aetna Insurance, Pacific Telesis, and the U.S. Army Recruiting Command. He currently consults on a variety of research and advisory projects in advertising and marketing, including advertising media plans for class-action lawsuits. He has also conducted research for a variety of enterprises including the U.S. Department of Health, Education and Welfare; the International Association of Business Communicators; and National Liberty Life Insurance.

Dr. Jugenheimer is author or coauthor of twenty books and many articles and papers. He has spoken before a variety of academic and professional organizations, including the World Advertising Congress in Tokyo. He also served as President and as Executive Director of the American Academy of Advertising and as Advertising Division Head of the Association for Education in Journalism and Mass Communication. He was Business Manager for the founding of the *Journal of Advertising*. He has testified about advertising before the U.S. House of Representatives Armed Forces Committee as well as in federal and state court proceedings.

Since earning his doctorate in Communications from the University of Illinois with a specialization in advertising and a minor in marketing, Dr. Jugenheimer has been a tenured faculty member at the University of Kansas, Louisiana State University (where he was the first person to hold the Manship Distinguished Professorship in Journalism), Fairleigh Dickinson University, Southern Illinois University, and Texas Tech University. At most of these universities, he also served as an administrator. He earned a bachelor's degree in advertising with a minor in economics and a master's degree in advertising with a minor in marketing from the University of Illinois at Urbana-Champaign. He worked at several adverting agencies in Chicago and downstate Illinois. He also served in the U.S. Air Force, first in aeromedical evacuation and later as a medical administrative officer.

Dr. Jugenheimer has lectured and conducted workshops in several countries and served on the guest faculty of the Executive Media MBA program for the Turku School of Economics and Business Administration in Finland. In addition, he has held a Kellogg National Fellowship. He is listed in *Who's Who in America, Who's Who in Advertising, Who's Who in Education,* and several other biographical references.

Dr. Jugenheimer is currently a partner and principal in the research, writing, and consulting firm In-Telligence, which concentrates on communications, marketing, and advertising.